THE MYSTERY OF BIRTH AND DEATH

Redefining the Self

D1600622

RAMTHA

THE MYSTERY OF BIRTH AND DEATH
Redefining the Self

Second Edition

JZK Publishing
A Division of JZK, Inc.

THE MYSTERY OF BIRTH AND DEATH
Redefining the Self
Second Edition

This book is a revised edition of *The Mystery of Birth and Death, Redefining the Self,* originally published in 2000 by JZK Publishing.

The contents of this book are based on Ramtha Dialogues®, a series of audio recordings registered with the United States Copyright Office, with permission of JZ Knight and JZK, Inc. The original audio recordings of the teachings of Ramtha used in the creation of this book are the following:

The Plateau for Learning (Audiotape-268, November 7, 1989. Copyright (P) 1989 JZ Knight), *Update on Change* (Audiotape-302, January 9, 1991. Copyright (P) 1991 JZ Knight), *Only One Thing* (Audiotape-336, September 19, 1996. Copyright (P) 1996 JZ Knight), *The Plane of Bliss, Part I* (CD-9703 and CD-9703.1, January 24-26, 1997. Copyright (P) 1997 JZ Knight), *The Plane of Bliss, Part II* (CD-9716, August 8-10, 1997. Copyright (P) 1997 JZ Knight).

Ramtha®, Ramtha Dialogues®, C&E®, Consciousness & Energy®, Fieldwork®, The Tank®, Blue Body®, Twilight®, Torsion Process®, Neighborhood Walk®, Mind As Matter®, Create Your Day®, Become a Remarkable Life®, The Grid®, Analogical Archery^{SM}, and Gladys® are trademarks and service marks of JZ Knight and are used with permission.

Cover design by Melissa Peizer

For more information about Ramtha's teachings, contact:

RAMTHA'S SCHOOL OF ENLIGHTENMENT
P.O. Box 1210,
Yelm, WA, 98597 USA
360.458.5201
800.347.0439
www.ramtha.com

ISBN # 978-157873-1220

JZK Publishing
A Division of JZK, Inc.
www.ramtha.com

Weary with toil, I haste me to my bed,
    The dear repose for limbs with travel tired;
But then begins a journey in my head,
To work my mind, when body's work's expired:
For then my thoughts (from far where I abide)
Intend a zealous pilgrimage to thee,
And keep my drooping eyelids open wide,
Looking on darkness which the blind do see:
Save that my soul's imaginary sight
Presents thy shadow to my sightless view,
Which, like a jewel hung in ghastly night,
Makes black night beauteous, and her old face new.
    Lo, thus, by day my limbs, by night my mind
    For thee, and for myself, no quiet find.

— *William Shakespeare*
Sonnet XXVII

CONTENTS

ACKNOWLEDGMENTS   8

INTRODUCTION: RAMTHA'S BOOK OF THE DEAD AND OF THE LIVING   9

CHAPTER 1
THE WHEEL OF REINCARNATION   17

Our Choices Before We Were Born   18

Living in the Past   22

The Path to Illumination   24

The Shadow Aspect of the Self   35

CHAPTER 2
THE ART OF DETACHMENT AND UNCONDITIONAL LOVE   41

It Is Possible to Own It All in One Lifetime   47

Ramtha's Learning to Detach from His Physical Body   50

The Egyptian Book of the Dead   53

The Importance of Change for the Soul's Journey   55

CHAPTER 3
THE LAST BATTLE AGAINST TYRANNY AND SLAVERY   61

The Conquest of Our Personal Limitations   62

Vision of the Collapse of Human Consciousness   65

Strategy to Preserve the Truth of Our Divine Inheritance   69

Using Emotional Energy As a Tool for Change   73

CHAPTER 4
REDEFINING THE SELF AS THE SPIRITUAL SELF   81

Abolition of the Self through Blame and Victimization   82
The Dark Night of the Soul   87
Judgment Day and the Life Review   90
Mapping Our New Life on the Plane of Bliss   95
The Value of Experiencing a New Incarnation   102

CHAPTER 5
MAKING THE CHOICE THAT ENDURES INTO ETERNITY   107

The Animal Nature of Humanity   108
Redefining the Self by Choosing Our Spiritual Nature   113
The Spiritual Walk of the Master   117
Resolution, a Spiritual Revolution   129
Practical Application and Instructions from Ramtha   141

CHAPTER 6
DEATH AND THE REVELATION OF OUR ULTERIOR MOTIVE 147

Revelation of Our Ulterior Motive   148
Freedom from the Deceit of the Past   161
Being an Honorable and Impeccable Person   168
Could It Be That You Are Already Dead?   171
Do We Choose Our Parents in Our Next Reincarnation?   178
Near-Death Experiences and the Egyptian Rites of Passage 188

CHAPTER 7
WHEN YOU LOVE YOURSELF ENOUGH   195

To a Master There Is No Birth and Death, Only Creation   196
Our Heart Weighed Against a Feather   207
Common Thought Is What Creates Our Daily Life   212
You Are Gods, the Creators of Reality   218
Engaging the Life Review Now through the Great Work   221
Triumph Over Death and the Alchemy of Transmutation   229

CLOSING WORDS: LIVING AS MULTIDIMENSIONAL BEINGS 235

EPILOGUE: AN INTRODUCTION TO RAMTHA'S TEACHINGS   243
SOURCES   253
RAMTHA'S SELECTED GLOSSARY   254
BIBLIOGRAPHY   258

ACKNOWLEDGMENTS

Our sincere thanks and appreciation to everyone who jointly helped bring about this book. It was an arduous teamwork effort inspired by the same love we all share for our Master Teacher, Ramtha, and his words.

We would like to acknowledge Debbie Christie for making the original words of Ramtha available for transcription. We appreciate the literary and copy editing work of Patricia Richker and Jaime Leal-Anaya. It was very exciting to translate the core of Ramtha's message into visual form through the inspiration of artist Melissa Peizer. Finally, we would like to extend our appreciation and love to JZ Knight for her unfaltering dedication to the Great Work and for making Ramtha's teachings available to everyone who wants to hear them and conquer themselves into enlightenment.

INTRODUCTION: RAMTHA'S BOOK OF THE DEAD AND OF THE LIVING

The other side of death has been a great unknown, a cold and bitter mystery for most people in our civilization today. Many experience it as an inevitable destiny and a frightening end. It is a great unknown, with many common elements shared across borders, religions, and cultures around the world. Its anticipated imagery has undoubtedly become deeply ingrained in our modern culture, in literature, movies, works of art, well beyond the religious domain.

The pictures of life after death inspired by religion — especially Christianity's vision of heaven and hell — are culturally shared by believers and nonbelievers alike. They can become truly morbid, macabre, gory, and chilling if you find yourself guilty and in disfavor from the Church, unfit according to religious laws to live with God in its heavenly abode. We can see a clear example of this in Hyeronimous Bosch's representation of hell and the torments of eternal damnation portrayed in his famous painting, "The Garden of Earthly Delights."

The sharp blade of doubt and fear, when death seems to come near, often cuts and bends the knee of even the staunchest materialist or disbeliever, just in case maybe they might have been wrong. Fear — fear of death, fear of the unknown — is always strongest and the most oppressive in the absence of knowledge. The divine torch of knowledge dispels the darkness of fear and brings forth newness and life, whereas the fear of knowledge is the worst enslavement and self-punishment that keeps us ignorant, superstitious, and dead in our tracks.

This was not the case in the ancient world, in places like Egypt, where they had knowledge, art, and ritual about the afterlife known today as the Book of the Dead. The Tibetans in the Far East and the Mayas in ancient Yucatan also had their own versions and instructions for crossing death's threshold to life on the other side. The problem we face today is that we no longer have the proper tools and context of interpretation to understand these books and rituals of the dead anymore. The rise of Judaism out of Egypt and, later, Christianity took care of destroying and burying the great ancient wisdom of Egypt under the desert sands. The situation became grimmer when they adapted and distorted much of the Egyptian tradition and knowledge in a fanatical and materialistic way, without any understanding at all.

One of the most ancient and important Egyptian stories, the story of Isis and the birth of Horus — the true, divine son, heir to the throne, and future wise ruler — morphed and changed into the story of Mary, the virgin mother of Jesus, the only son of God, and King of Kings. This is one of the clearest examples that shows the tragic destruction and distortion of fundamental, ancient Egyptian traditions. Even traditional, Christian art representing the virgin mother and the son of God on her lap is identical to the original works from ancient Egypt representing Isis and her son Horus on her loving lap thousands of years prior to Christianity. How can this be? What was the purpose of copying and distorting this original, sacred imagery? And what was the original knowledge and wisdom of the Egyptians that got covered up, obscured, and lost through the Judeo-Christian editing and appropriation process?

We need to find the answers to these questions if we want to understand correctly the instructions in the original Egyptian Book of the Dead that have remained so mysterious and impenetrable. It could possibly also shed light on many other sacred texts that came after. In order to truly decipher this knowledge, we must really think and walk as an ancient Egyptian. We cannot attempt to read and interpret ancient knowledge with our modern thinking, using our current views, beliefs, and understanding of reality. It does not work. It is an all-too-common mistake, unfortunately. We need someone to guide and help us understand the ideas and mind of the ancient world and give us an insight into its ancient wisdom.

Ramtha and his teachings have offered us such help and insight over four decades now, and counting. Simply his story of creation of the Void contemplating itself — and the first point of consciousness that emerged, the legendary Point Zero, and the journey of involution and evolution through seven levels of consciousness and energy — this story alone shines a bright light of understanding and removes the paradoxical contradictions and occult mysteries that are inherent in so many traditional stories of creation. Not only does he ground his teachings in ancient wisdom but goes to great lengths to dispel the darkness of superstition by using current, common, scientific concepts that anyone can relate to, understand, and put to the test to verify the teachings personally.

In regard to our quest into the afterlife and the instructions in the Book of the Dead to safely journey there, we are in the company of a great expert and knowledgeable source. Ramtha often explains that his teachings are indeed the resurrection of what once was the ancient knowledge and wisdom of Egypt, now long gone:

"In ancient Egypt the Pharaoh was a servant to the people. And everyone could read. Everyone had access to the secret mysteries. Everyone participated in the building of the icons and the symbolism of their own thought. There was no such thing that women were subjected to men. Did you know where that idea came from? It came from the latter-day Jews, that women would become filthy and unclean, but in ancient Egypt they were considered Winged Pharaohs of the Gods. They were nearer to God. To have a woman in your life was to be nearer to God, for their wisdom and their virtue were worth in our manly kingdom an instantaneous gratification, and saved our kingdom."

"In ancient Egypt, the Pharaoh was the people. All of the people could read and write, and all the people had access to all of the great temples of worship. They had access to all of the priests. And that was overturned with the desert princes of Abraham, the Hittite kingdom, that came and conquered them and slaughtered them and rose themselves up in a masculine point of view and subdued the women forever and ever and ever. I want you to know that, yes, there is a resurrection of the ancient religion of Egypt and you are looking at it right here and now."[1]

— Ramtha

Ramtha makes two very important points for us here: Everyone in Egypt in those ancient times had equal access to the divine and to the sacred knowledge. He also makes the point that women were not subjected to men and were not considered unequal. Women were revered for their wisdom and virtue. They were considered divine beings and an asset

---

1 Ramtha, *Revolution of the Spirit and Mammy, the Goddess of Genesis.* Audiotape 444 edition. March 10, 2000 (Yelm: Ramtha Dialogues®, 2000); also in Ramtha, *A Master's Reflection on the History of Humanity, Part II, Rediscovering the Pearl of Ancient Wisdom,* Second Edition (Yelm: JZK Publishing, 2017).

to everyone in the kingdom. Women today are often still not considered equal, for example, when it comes to their pay in the workplace, and they continue to be excluded from positions of leadership and authority in many world religions and politics. Why are these points important? What does this have to do with life after death? Their significance can easily escape us. But it really boils down to how we view ourselves, how we define ourselves. Who are we, and thus who is the one that gets to live and die, and who or what survives the death of the body and continues on? If we still struggle with gender equality and one gender is greater and above the other, then it essentially means that we have — perhaps unconsciously — reduced ourselves and defined our essence in terms of male and female and the physical body. This is the first golden key we must keep close in our exploration, a most important master key that opens hidden doors to new understanding, as you will see.

In Ramtha's teachings and in ancient Egypt, human beings — regardless of gender, social status, age, or creed — are acknowledged as divine beings, sovereign entities, Gods and creators of reality and destiny by virtue of their common thoughts and mind. One of the reasons why religion has so little wisdom to offer us today, and so much superstition fills in that vacant place, is precisely because the essence of a human being is commonly seen in terms of its physical image, its body, and its attributes. Precisely because God's divine qualities and divine knowledge as creators and source of our life are not included in our definition of who we are by nature, then it inevitably follows that we are separated from God, wholly helpless and fragile creatures condemned to a mortal life.

How interesting that two apparently simple and unrelated things — gender equality and direct access to God — can have such a fundamental impact in how we view ourselves and the potential destiny we can expect and accept in life and afterlife. It is the body, after all, that is seen in lore and religions ascending to heaven and receiving the ultimate price of eternal bliss, and it is the body that is perceived descending to hell and eternal torment and punished with a horrible fate. But we are not the body. We are not reduced to our physical embodiment and our gender expression and are not cut off from direct access to the divine because we are made of the divine itself, endowed with the gift of free will, free choice, and the ability of free thought and reason. That is who we really are and what makes us remarkable humans and truly divine. From the beginning of his message when he first appeared in the late 1970s, Ramtha emphatically and lovingly insists: "Behold God. You are Gods, creators of your destiny, the forgotten Gods."

The instructions of the Book of the Dead were not intended for the physical body, embalmed and buried in a lavish tomb, but for the living God that gave it life, that imbued its embodiment with a warm touch and a sparkle in its eyes. Ramtha explains:

> "The Egyptian Book of the Dead is to teach the sovereign what to do the moment it is out of its body: what to say, where to go, who to see, what to do. They are enchanted with it. Why are the priests saying prayers twenty-four hours a day reciting those passages, reciting them over and over and over? Because that priest is in the light review of that sovereign. That priest is praying for that sovereign, and that sovereign in the light review is hearing the priest from the other side. Don't you understand?"[2]

> — Ramtha

---

2 Ramtha, *The Plane of Bliss, Part II.* CD-9716 edition, August 8-10, 1997 (Yelm: Ramtha Dialogues®, 1997).

14

When our essence and identity, the self, is defined in terms of our free will, our thoughts, our choices rather than reduced to our body, we begin to understand the physical body for what it really is. It is the garment, the spacesuit that we wear, the vehicle we need in order to experience the realities we create in our life. The concept of reincarnation, the immortality of the soul or Spirit, and life after death can now begin to gain new meaning and clarity against this frame. We can now begin to understand who it is that survives physical death and who has the ability to continue on to life after life or return to a new vehicle of life incarnate, a new life's reincarnation into flesh and blood, if you wish, or go onto a future beyond and unknown as the divine son and daughter of the invisible God we really are and always have been unto forever.

In this book, we prepared for you Ramtha's classic teachings where he delves deeply into these arcane mysteries of life and death, the afterlife and the life review in the light, reincarnation, how we get to choose our parents and our future incarnation, weighed in by the unfinished business recorded by our soul that we set out to make known and own into wisdom before we were born. Ramtha explains the place of rest where we meet other beings like us on the other side and how we get to plan our next move on the plane of demonstration. He gives us suggestions and the options we could call upon if we are cloaked with knowledge and know how to speak and ask and how to visualize and plan our great evolutionary, future destiny.

What is perhaps most important in this teaching by Ramtha are the details he discloses of how masters, immortal masters, do not have to wait to die to plan their next life or to own as wisdom what is still undone in their soul. How is it they speak, even if death were to take them by surprise? These are truly great, arcane secrets laid bare in the open for all of us to learn and see.

They are truly the golden, rose rays of a new morning's rising sun, the master keys of wise masters who found the secret of life and conquered death. That is why we call these teachings "Ramtha's Great Book of the Dead and of the Living." As you continue to read, do not forget the two points Ramtha reminded us from the ancient Egyptians: Men and Women are Gods equivalent, divine creators of morning's destiny in death and life.

To your great life!

— *Jaime Leal-Anaya*
Editor and Writer, JZK Publishing

Chapter 1
The Wheel of Reincarnation

> *"This thread or this shadow self is the self*
> *that holds the burden as well as the power of*
> *victimization — reaction, hate, resentment,*
> *bitterness, jealousy, anger, all of those pitiful*
> *emotions that do nothing but destroy the health of*
> *the body — and causes you to have to come back*
> *again and to address those issues with the same*
> *people in a future state."*
>   *— Ramtha*

Our Choices Before We Were Born

O my beloved God,
of this day
I have contemplated
my spiritual growth.
As of this night
I desire to know
where I am in my growth.
I beseech you
to send to me a sign,
that this sign
will read to me
the level of my growth
and indeed the level
of my spiritual acceptance.
So be it.

Now we are going to have a wonderful teaching this evening because it has already happened. I know it was wonderful. This wonderful ability to be able to already know that is because I can watch several scenes unfold and, as a strategist, be able to choose different scenes from different times of this same evening, answer questions differently, teach differently, and send specific runners. And I am very happy to say it was all a success. When you are on top of the mountain, you get a different view of things than when you are down in the valley and you can't see anything.

I am going to start by reminding you of an event, and in its curious statement it will say a great deal about who you are.

After this teaching is over I want you to ponder this, and I want you to ponder it deeply and richly. The event is that before you incarnated into this lifetime — before this life, before this body — you already had the option to be here, and you elected to be here because it was part of your soul's journey. All of you — from all times, all cultures, and all peoples — before you were born again had to have an agenda for life; otherwise that life wouldn't unfold. And in that agenda all of you elected to find me in this school.

I want you to think about that, because it begs the question if this was part of my soul's journey in making it here and studying, then what specifically was it that I needed to know to satisfy the requirement of the lords of karma and reincarnation? In other words, what would I gain from coming here that would satisfy this nagging problem that I seem to carry into each life, stumble through it, die in that life, and still carry the same problem? What is it that this school and this Teacher have to offer me?

This is what I want you to know. In everything that you have learned in my audience and all the runners and all the teachings that I have given you, you have made lifetime leaps in knowledge and experiences. Let me specify by saying that those lifetime leaps have nothing to do with affecting material form — that is to come — but have everything to do with affecting the state of your spiritual self, in evolving it through a brain/body connection in a lifetime to a level of understanding that allows that Spirit and soul to move very quickly through the veils of lifetimes.

In other words, we cannot measure yet what it is that you have gained, but understanding knowledge — an enriched experience — brings about wisdom. When given the opportunity, you can rise to the occasion and address life's situations not from a common, impoverished state of social consciousness that is always blaming someone or something for the condition of one's life — in particular your own — but you can address situations in your life without being the victim. You can address it in such an enriched manner that you stand in awe of the wisdom that starts to flow out of you, and it speaks of a learning capacity you have gained that you did not always have.

Why is that important? Because we — myself included — who elected in life to know everything and to find that there were no borders or parameters to the unknown, and chose to live exclusively on a path that would always take us into the unknown, were called the masters. We were called the great ones because we dared to learn more about that which is termed self than the common rabble of the marketplace did. Masters must have the ability to understand their lives, understand nature, and understand and take responsibility for their actions in nature before the full, forthwith power of manipulating mass is given to them.

That is why I tell you that you came here and are all here because you wanted to be here. And what you have learned thus far, though not visible, is building that which is termed a bounty inside of you of tremendous knowledge. If we can continue to refine that knowledge and remove from it the silliness and immature qualities of victimization, past problems, someone else's fault — if we can continue to polish this understanding down to the present moment of self, which we are endeavoring to do — when we enter that sanctuary where what we are is no one else's responsibility in any area of our life except our own and we finally come to that bare arena is the moment we become utterly and fantastically empowered as lawgivers. But it does not come until we can enter that place naked — naked of our past, blame, envy, jealousy — naked of everything that plagues human consciousness and keeps it submissive to social consciousness. Then we are polishing attitudes to a system of knowledge that blames no one, that lives in no time other than Now, and indeed from that basis grows strong roots into the Void with tremendous power.

You wanted to know what you have come here to learn. There are no accidents in life; everything is intentional. Let us say that maybe the reason you have been recycled in the engines of reincarnation over and over and over is because there is one flaw in your thinking, and that flaw can be one little thing or event, one small attitude. Why would that be a flaw? Why would that be like a rope that anchors you into lifetime after lifetime addressing the same issue? No matter in what culture you are born, in what time you are born — no matter what color your skin or if you are rich or poor — it doesn't matter; you still are plagued with this same little problem. Perhaps that is the only thing that brought you back here other than studying in this school, and perhaps in this study you will find the solution.

Karma and the lords of karma, I liked battling with them because they wield an enormous power of suppression. But what karma really means is that what you think, you are; what you think, you create. Thinking must be that pure and that clear so if you think badly and do badly to someone else, that bad will be done back to you because that is experiencing the reality that you are meting out. Karma can be such a suppressing concept that instead of creating masters, it can absolutely destroy minds that are working toward greatness by taking from them every sweet thing that life has to offer: living in a monastic style of life and charting the course of their thinking in endless mantras that mean nothing; prostrating the body and starving the body; doing every possible thing to avoid the encounter of potential karma, even with eyesight. Now that is rather extreme.

Let me tell you that there is no one event in your life that you have that keeps you on the cycle of reincarnation that cannot be resolved when you polish the attitude and slough off of it people, places, things, events, and time. That is going naked into the center of an attitude. When you can do that with any problem that you have is the only time you will ever resolve it. Blaming your parents, blaming a time, being victimized by an event, all of those are actions upon a reaction that keep you coming back. And the solution is so utterly simple: See it for what it is without any dressings, including the past. And if you are able to do that, then you will know what sort of substantive entity you are that can look in the eye of your necromancer until the veil is lifted and you find that the necromancer has no face.

Living in the Past

What your difficulty is and has always been is that you live in a past hurt and a past grievance. I don't know how many times I have to say this, but even my most advanced group still digs up reasons in their past for their behavior, and digging up old corpses is only going to make the situation stink. That does not resolve anything. What it does do is connect you to those same people for another lifetime to come. Why do you think there are soul groups that work together? There is such a thing. There are groups in this very audience. And of course the larger group has a soul connection in my lifetime. We were all together one time. But in the time span from then to now, you have all had little dramas in your life that you do to one another. And whoever you lay the blame on in this lifetime for your present misery is exactly who you are going to get the next lifetime.

Now think about that. Is that not logical to you? If

consciousness and energy create reality through the processes of the brain and its neuronet mapping, and your neuronet says that you are weak because of your parents and that becomes unresolved in this lifetime and they are always held to that issue, is not then consciousness and energy creating that as absolute reality? Would not then that reality be carried over into another experience with the same people? Yes, because they are in your reality. How does it escape being stripped at the light? Only the memory is stripped at the light but the soul, the page that hasn't had anything recorded on it for thousands of years, begs for resolution because for thousands of years you are stuck in one little attitude. That is lack.

Now great beings all know this and very soon you are going to know that. You are going to know it because I am going to press to you that realization and its profound implications for your future Now. And I want to do that because as long as you play with the idea of suffering through a person, place, event, or time, then you and that suffering and that entity will be bound together for all eternity until one day you give it up.

Now this has great implications — great implications — because it shows the level of immaturity in a school of ancient wisdom. No master will ever, ever blame his or her life. No master will ever lay the power of his or her fall or rise at the feet of any other individual or any event or any time. That is how you know you are talking to a true master of the Great Work.

Is it possible to really change the way your brain thinks by focusing on this little problem of yours without connecting it to all of these other forms that are common in association to the problem? Absolutely, because when you focus on what it is — not who made it, when it happened, who caused it, and why you are in the days to follow progressively a certain way — when those are eliminated you are looking at a naked concept in the brain. Do you not know what that causes the brain to do? Now we have an unplugging of the neurons from their dendrite stations because if we focus on what we are without association, the brain must comply to be able to understand what it is you are doing, and they have to unplug the circuitry of association and give you simply what it is. And when you stare at what it is without association, it can no longer be. It is by virtue of association that it exists in the first place. You cannot sustain lack in any form when you have detached the associations with it and from it.

Now the quickest road to enlightenment is not drugs and is not wine. It is not anything outside of what we are. The most rapid road to mastery is the road of detachment. What that means is to detach from all mental, limited attitudes of blame — time, people, place, events — because when you take lack and stand it on its own, it cannot sustain without blame. And hate cannot live — hate cannot be sustained — unless it has a victim. Detach the victim and there is no hate. Detach from lack your job, the place you live, how much money you make. Detach from lack any perceived abilities of yours that would prevent abundance from occurring. If you detached all of that and simply looked at lack, it could not exist in your reality, because in a state of pure detachment we have the pure, present moment that is the most awesome power there is.

The Path to Illumination

My beloved people, illumination is a very old word, indeed it is a very powerful word, and it was only respected in very, very few people. They were often called prophets and wise men and women. They were very rare so they were very special and always sought out. But illumination here is being taught in the school. So what sort of person does it take to become illuminated or to begin the path of illumination? It takes the following person: one who is ready and willing to have owned all of their past. As a matter of fact, there is nothing from their past that beckons to them any longer. They have done it all. They accomplished all of their dreams. They had all their riches. They had all their poverty. They had everything. They were lovers, husbandmen and wives, hetaerae. They had done it all. And there came a moment in their lives that they were ready for something else. They wanted it, so the master appeared.

When one no longer yearns for their past, what does that have to say about the person? The person owns nothing and is owned by nothing — owned by nothing. Now that is a very broad statement. Here you are endeavoring to accumulate things and I am telling you it is about one who owns nothing. What does that really mean? It means there is nothing from the past that they are indebted to — indebted to not simply by gold but through grief and emotional adherence.

Now, second, the person who is ready for illumination is an entity that is willing to have an attitude diversely different than their past. Attitude — an attitude — is a very powerful word because the old ways of thinking no longer are recognized in a new attitude. An attitude that is brand-new is sort of like a brain born into this life that has had no programming done to it. It is an organism that is mature, but virtuous. What does that mean, a virtuous attitude? It means an attitude that is not filled up, one that is vacant — a nothing attitude, if you will. It seems impossible what it took a person who has lived many, many years to come to a point to have a nothing attitude. But when the person is no longer owned by yesterday, number one, when there is nothing that beckons to them — there are no dreams, there is no obligation, there is nothing owned and nothing owing — when that is accomplished the person has a virgin attitude, and that attitude then is ripe for development.

To be God exemplified is to be illuminated in the most profound sense of the word, being in knowledge of, and then aggressively experiencing that knowledge. This new attitude has room, if you will, as a new consciousness to absorb knowledge and then with such dynamic focus to create the knowledge as one's daily life to engage in and indeed to fulfill. This new consciousness is not judgmental, is not biased, is no longer prejudiced, is no longer devoted, as it were, to demigods. It is devoted to God Almighty, the sovereign potential. This virgin attitude has no need to gossip. This virgin attitude has no need to be a dictator, has no need to be a victim. This new attitude has no need for further bodily sensations because the virgin consciousness has become that way by the person owning their past.

Next, third, is that life is forever — life is forever. Everyone can say that in this audience. But an individual who can reckon that the potential of their eternal self exists beyond some veil — the mere fact they know that they are eternal — then no longer do they have fear. They realize they are eternal and hunger for that and conceptualize that their eternalness is behind some veil. It is through them they will lift the veil, because in order to think in those terms one must not be afraid to die. When you are no longer afraid to die, then the concept of eternal life is ever-present.

So what is that quality? What does that mean to you? What could you possibly do to walk on an edge and not lose anything? To be fearless is to no longer fear death, therefore no longer fearing changes into the unknown. Most of you are very frightened about the unknown. That is a difficult quality and one of the reasons that you do not manifest very well. A person who indeed engages that which is termed eternal life no longer considers death and no longer considers age because they become ageless in the light of all eternity. So if a person no longer fears death then what would they fear? They have no fear of public ostracism. They have no fear of social rebuke. They have no fear of being either famous or unknown. And in most senses the great initiate does not seek to be known because that had everything to do with yesterday. You understand now?

So what are the three? Owning the past, having a new attitude, and life is forever. Those are the makings of a Christ. That is the reason why the illuminated ones were so rare in antiquity because look at what they had to become, not forcibly but what was a natural evolution in them. Now let's take and put that initiate into engaging Consciousness & Energy®.[3] When that initiate forms the picture of its want — its discipline is so aligned that its breath is conscious power — when they engage a word they are absolute Now. They have no fear of winning or losing. Winning and losing don't exist because they have a new consciousness. And in eternity, to live forever, this is a sign of that eternalness so they have passion. They are not sitting here thinking about someone else. They are not sitting here thinking about how they look, what they are going to do tomorrow, what they did yesterday. They are not sitting here afraid of what will happen when they engage this word. They are not afraid of what people will think once they manifest it. They are absolute. And there are a few of you in this audience that are all of these things I have just listed and you are the manifesters. So when you blow it out, it is absolute law because there is no fear it will manifest or that it won't manifest.

---

3 See the Glossary for more information on Ramtha's discipline of Consciousness & Energy® (C&E®).

Now let's take the next group who are having some difficulties over here. If the true initiate possesses these three qualities, what would be the indicators of one who longs for knowledge and illumination but who has not quite gotten there? They live in the past and are still fighting with their image. They have not learned that they have already been this image. They have not learned that it is enough, that time is over with being this identity. So they live not only in the past but they do so through the activity of their image. And what is that? That has everything to do with yesterday, today, and tomorrow. It has everything to do with your sexuality. It has everything to do with your relationship. It has everything to do with how you look and how you don't look. It has everything to do with living to public approval. It has everything to do with running away from adversity. It has everything to do with being small-minded.

The second one is an attitude. What is the attitude of one who has not quite arrived? The attitudes of these people are still judgmental. Their bodies rule their lives: what is between their legs, on their chest, how many muscles or how few muscles, and who sleeps in their bed and who doesn't sleep in their bed. These people judge people and as a result they are judged. These people have a fear, if you will, always of not doing the right thing. And whoever determined what the right thing was? The image is what determined the right thing, and always you did the wrong thing trying to do the right thing. These people's possessions have great worth, no matter how small or how large. It is all relative. And these people, above all, do not like to be alone.

And, third, what about the veil of eternity? What is it with this particular group? They are afraid of death. They are afraid of pain. They are afraid to suffer. If you are afraid of pain and suffering and you are afraid of dying asleep, unawakened, you are afraid because both of these lead to the ultimate pain, death.

Where is the veil of eternity to them? They can hack someone's head off and watch the blood spew out of the neck and say, see, this person is dead. Where is the Spirit? Where is their consciousness? They are dead and gone. These people have a mechanical mind that is frosted with mysticism. They know you die but hope to God they are saved.

Now these people not only are afraid of death. That ultimate fear mirrors everything up to them, that the basis of everything in their life is from the motivation of fear. And how is their image lived all this time? They are afraid it wouldn't please, because if it doesn't please it is ostracized, and if it is ostracized it will suffer emotionally, and if it suffers emotionally it will die as a manic depressive or its heart will break.

So why do some of you get the opposite when you blow it out? Because you are in the second group. Now that is not a derogatory statement. That is a fact. And the fact is that you have not come to that epic point of cleansing, to that new consciousness of what is truly important in your life. And love doesn't rule your life because you have not earned the right to have it. Only the initiate possesses that golden thread called love. It is not the love between two people. It is the ultimate love of God, which is the whole of the All that is in the All — everything.

So why is it you engaged joy and in the beginning you started to suffer and everything started going wrong? Why is it that you engaged sovereignty and suddenly started losing everything? And why is it that you engaged health and suddenly started getting sicker? You are the second category. The reason for this is that your sincerity and your commitment to change and the glory of transformation cannot occur until the fracturing, if you will, of that which is termed the past, the fracturing and the cracking of the mirror of imagery, the cracking and the peeling of fear is done out of your life. So when you ask for joy, what begins to happen is everything from your subconscious, from your image, begins to surface. In order for the God to have sovereignty of joy, it must clean out its cabinet and burnish its shelves that a brilliant, illuminated thing can rest there in glory.

So when you engage joy, you are going to engage misery, pain and suffering, and you are going to have to make decisions because these are the things that hold you in the past and indeed define your image of need. So here they come one by one. And you are suffering and you are confused and indeed you are hurting and it is not happening the way you thought. But joy cannot live in the same body as pain. Joy cannot share a throne with the past because the past is not joyous, only the Now. So here they come: things you did, people you blamed. All that unworthiness starts to come up. And no matter if anyone buys you a pretty present, you cannot even feel the glee and the zest of its wrapping, and you are hurting.

Now let me tell you, masters, I understand this very well because such was my life. Joy cannot make you anew unless you make you anew. The conquest of self is all about conquering the limitations of the individual classified as a past person, fracturing all of the bigotry, all of the hate, the injustice, all of the dishonesty. It fractures everything and brings it to the surface. The mirror of the image cracks. So one by one they come up, and they are the issues that manifest — not joy. You see, the way to the kingdom of heaven is to make your path straight.

If you are to start this day to be the illuminated one where truly you possess the qualities of a rare initiate, you who are in second running must do all of this. You must rejoice somewhere that this is occurring, that you too one day shall have the clarity and a new consciousness and an eternalness of being that would allow the miracles to be created, in a twinkling of an eye, that powerful and that pure. Your road is very difficult because everything that you endeavor to manifest you are going to have to clean the way for its appearance, and that every depression, with every sorrow, with every weakness you are to forge the sword that will cause you indeed to master yourself. That is what they said to me, "Here, Ram, conquer yourself." Yes, I did.

So what do you do when you are in the midst of sadness and you want joy? What do you do? Do you have self-pity that you bathe in? Do you go and discuss this with your friends so that they can bathe you some more? Do you call everyone on the tele and tell them about your anguish? Are they going to help you? I have listened to you. They are not going to help you. What do you do? You take the second, most powerful learning of the first initiate, a new consciousness. Instead of seeing this as "Woe is me, I ask for joy but got suffering so I am unworthy of it" — that is yesterday's news, the old dictum, the old reply, the old escape — the consciousness of the initiate, the new attitude, says, "Alas, I am finding my salvation, for indeed it is within me all along. This oppression that I feel, I know from whence it comes." And if you don't, you blow out oppression and the next part of the picture will appear until the solitary answer looms in front of you. All you have to do is bring it on, bring it on. Why? Bring it on and it will appear as magical in your life. In the form of people from the past, from the present, in the form of a thing, in the form of a letter, in the form of a word it will appear and then you will be illuminated and then you look at this with a new consciousness. You will say, "Ah, I am free at last, for now I understand." And with that glory and a great shout it is consumed into wisdom and evermore is the consciousness cleaned out of that ageless drama.

Then the next situation comes up, and instead of running from it you engage it with a sword, and the sword is Consciousness & Energy®. The new attitude says this is a blessing, this is clearing my path for the glory of God, and you engage it and you call it forward. You will know when your manifestation that you have arduously worked to achieve has manifested, for one sweet morn you will arise from your pallet and look upon that which is termed a morning sky, and in the twinkling of fading stars you will have a glee and a joy that will rise to its zenith. The sweetest of laughter will merge with the night bird's call, and the new day will be filled with a golden energy that everything that you see and touch will reflect the beauty of you. And, behold, you now know joy and you have labored for it — labored for it.

Now what have you done to the fractured image of the past? You have turned it into pearls. The mirror of the image is so fractured and distorted, there are remnants left and you bring them on. With each conquest you gain strength, and with strength comes courage, and with courage comes the birthing of a true initiate, and that birthing truly makes you free and you will never be the same ever again. Then when you go to sovereignty and see that you nigh have not a pence, rejoice that you have not a pence. And if only bread have you for your supper and your heart begins to weep, is it weeping for the frugalness of what you sup or are you weeping for those who have less? And sovereignty begins to be engaged the same way joy is. It does not always take gold to be sovereign. It takes strength and courage and an unlimited mind to create, and the good earth and the sweetness of life will provide the moment you engage.

And you go to health. Why is health the last? Because health is a physical diseasement or that which is termed a bodily affliction, whether it is age, it is deterioration of that which is termed tissue, or disease is set upon you, and the body is falling under the siege. Why should health be the last? Because health, as it were, is a physical manifestation, and physical manifestation is equal to that which is termed the last straws of creation. It will manifest in the body. The body lives in time. It has its own rhythm. It has its own electrum. It has its own individual function. It is an instrument of that which is termed this plane. The body will suffer or rejoice at creativity of joy, of the image, of sovereignty, of poverty. The body will rejoice or weep under the attitude of you who inhabit it.

Now it is the last straw of everyone's creation — the physical. So how do you blow out the word health and get sicker? If the body manifests illness in the face of engaging the manifestation called health, then what the body is telling you in its language is it can only talk to you through pain or gas or a cramp or a weakness or a soreness, a blowing up, or losing it all. The body talks to you every single day and is trying to tell you something that you are doing to it. It needs help. If you are the Lord God of your being, if you are the supreme image of your being, then surely what must follow is that your physical body is the ultimate kingdom and indeed servant to either one. So your body talks to you.

If you are getting sicker and you are blowing out health, you must look at this in the new attitude of consciousness. This physical body is asking for help. That is its way of talking. Now it will start to show you what is wrong, and then you blow that out and find out the attitude that has created it. For every ache and pain and ailment and disease, there is an attitude that is reigning and riding sovereign over this body. Then you address the attitude with courage. And it is very simple to interpret. You need not be a genius — you may be a simpleton — to interpret what the body is trying to tell you. And at whatever part it is talking to you, it is very simple to recognize the attitude, indeed that which is termed the consciousness that is making this physical body malfunction. Then you engage every part. And then as it begins to hurt more, you engage the attitude or the language of the pain and it will reveal itself to you. Then you engage it and change it.

Now we come to the reason why people do not change, why people do not heal their bodies, because they are not willing to find the attitude that has crippled it. They do not want to change the attitude that they have found, indeed, that is their identity. If they lose their identity, indeed they lose their image. If they lose their image, indeed they lose the respect of their peers. If they lose the respect of their peers, they are unworthy. And if they are unworthy, they are afraid to die because there is no eternity for that misery.

So you want to heal your body? You must be willing to go into it and to talk to it. You must have the courage and the passion to change that which has put it into malfunction and misery, and you must be willing to change. And if that change is so complete, indeed so absolute that it destroys your past, then that malfunctioning body, indeed that disease, has then the epic blessing of your life because it will deliver you out of the bondage of an over-and-over-and-over-again human rut.

So Consciousness & Energy® works because the will truly exists. I can say to you the most courageous, esteemed, truly glorified saints that ever lived at most have never been recognized because they never sought notoriety. They suffered, they endured, for the sake of the glory of God manifesting in them, for the sake of illumination. And what courage was it in a Christ? What courage did it take to have nothing but to own it all? What courage did it take to be the only one in a hysterical mob that knew peace? What kind of courage does it take to be willing to die to show that life is forever? "Blessed be you, for you send me to my Father and free me of this world." So what kind of courage does it take to meet adversity and to rejoice and see the splendor in even a lily? What kind of greatness does it take? One that has been truly mastered and engaged. What kind of person who can walk alone and be alone in the midst of ten thousand strong, where does its comfort come from? From the glory of the Father within them, something they don't teach but live. That is the epic of illumination. And all the steps of these great, great people's lives were fraught, as it were, with change, and they had it in them to embrace it and change and grow and bloom. They are where you, pray be it so, can someday walk, because you have walked as one.

The Shadow Aspect of the Self

Many of you have what has been commonly referred to as a dark-sided character, which means the shadow aspect of you, a filament or a thread that is rough and raw. And that thread, I would best say, is a neuronet map. You covet this side of yourself so deliciously so as to never let anything penetrate it. This thread or this shadow self is the self that holds the burden as well as the power of victimization — reaction, hate, resentment, bitterness, jealousy, anger, all of those pitiful emotions that do nothing but destroy the health of the body — and causes you to have to come back again and to address those issues with the same people in a future state. That is nothing to look forward to. You have this side to your character that you protect, and you relish it and use it as a whip and a sting. It is an ugly, ugly aspect of yourself, and I see it in you.

All that it is, is a specific map that you have in your brain that you shield and protect. Only a master can see what is really sitting behind that sweet, little face. Most people are running around trying to put on a good face to hide this shadowy character of their personality, and because everyone is doing it, no one sees that everyone is that already.

Now let me tell you about that little character. That stubborn, altered-ego facet of the brain — that part of yourself that you refuse to let go — is guarded richly by having a life of its own because it can point to circumstances in its life that made it that way: betrayal, abandonment, being lied to, being used, abused, neglected, all of those words that you use so commonly in your dialogues with one another. This ugly, little altered ego that you possess has been the most difficult entity in this school to change because you don't want to change it, and I have given you the keys to do it. Why don't you want to change it? Because it affords you a battery of protection against people that you think are out to get you or take advantage of you. So it provides the sting, the venom, the ugliness, the manipulation, the resentment, the cleverness, and all the things that you found you needed for the sake of your own survival.

But let me tell you about this dark, little creature. Because of that entity you are going to miss the greatest message in this school that your soul brought you here to learn. When we dissolve the inner demon — that shadowy creature inside ourselves, like I did, laid down my broadsword — we do become vulnerable, but we become vulnerable only for the first moment of our fear of reprisal because we did so. And that is a useless fear in the face of knowledge.

What then holds your little demon together? Your nastiness of temper. You can say, "I have a bad temper because of this and this and this." But what if we removed that, would there still be a bad temper? No, there wouldn't. And what do we do with the bad-temper energy? It is free. It becomes free space.

What if then you say, "I don't trust people because I have

been betrayed." I would look at you and say, well, you are the first person you shouldn't trust because you are the greatest betrayer to yourself than anyone will ever be to you. And why is that? Because you have a guarded attitude and you refuse to neutralize the association to that attitude to be free of it. You see, trusting people only becomes an issue when you have difficulty trusting yourself. When there is no problem in self-trust, it never is an issue because there is no association there to cling to. What we begin to do is disarm — in the face of absolute power — a part of yourself that is really responsible for many, many wonderful things coming into your life that don't come because you always have this shield up and the shield never allows you to live in this moment. You are never really here with me; you are really back somewhere else in another time.

This little creature that you have inside of you — which was appropriately called the devil or the demon, the inner demon — is that person who has a whole storehouse of information about why they should be the way they should be. All that information is interlinked with many people and many places, many things and many events, but it is only one demon with many tentacles. And it takes a great amount of resistance to the beauty of life to feed the monster. For example, when I say resistance to life, I have people here who would rather hold onto that than dissolve it. How do I know that? Even in teaching you to move and simply look at what it is without the attachment of people, places, things, events, and time, some of you still went back to your past and still cling to that. Past association is an attachment. It is the only thing that supports that which doesn't really exist. Lack is an illusion. What is real is the attitude that supports it.

The mastery of oneself is a noble and worthwhile pursuit, but it is a pursuit that takes you into the inner corridors of yourself, as it were, and really makes you look at parts of yourself that so far have been your persona, the way people perceive you. And there is an element of fear that if you get rid of that persona, then people won't take you seriously or you won't be big and bad enough to make any difference, but that is a lie. As long as you dwell on an insignificant issue like a single attitude that has caused you to be born so many times — has ruined so many relationships, so many opportunities, so many days that came and are gone and will never be again, that ruined the landscape of life totally — as long as that remains in your life, the hope for future lives is very dim. And the ability to expressly be a master is vastly undermined by clinging to something that you just need to give up. It is a no-thing.

This is a diseasement in human consciousness. And, my beloved people, I want you to know that I am pressing you to that center arena, challenging and endeavoring to show you something so sweet and indeed so beautiful, that all the things of which you were afraid about yourself that you thought were the truth don't even exist. The only thing that exists is the association that you believe to be with them, and that association is what needs to be removed. Then there is no such thing as inadequacies or hate, and indeed there is no such thing as malice. There is no such thing as suffering and lack, and there is no such thing even as death. There really isn't.

If we think about this, your demons are really about your need to support your attitudes in order to make you survive, and yet they are the very attitudes that utterly cripple you from life. What is on the other side of that? I know a brave man. All I have to do is look at him and I can see in him that substance of quality that I know makes up bravery. Bravery isn't about being big, bad, and bold. Bravery is about the impeccable strength to cleave from oneself the cancerous thought that weakens an individual and his performance in life in every area. Now that is strength and it is also bravery.

I can tell by looking at a woman if there rests within that bosom sincere love and affection. Sincere love and affection are the utter embodiment of God, as the Goddess is indeed the nurturer of life and never the robber of it — the giver of love, never the mutilator of it — and in the woman we find God's sweetest flower. I can look at a woman and tell you whether that love abides there or not. What makes a woman beautiful is not the skin, the eyes, the age. What makes a woman beautiful is her capacity to love unyieldingly and to love without conditions. Now that is what I consider a beautiful woman.

Lack can be seen as a crystal ball propped up by that which is termed a triad of legs, and what is really seen here is not a crystal ball but the triad of legs that is propping it up. We could see lack then as a crystal transparent ball which we really can't see, but what we do see are the props that position it. The props of association are saying that you are the way you are because of what happened to you when you were a little girl or a little boy and carrying that all the way through your life and coloring every day of your life with it, for that is the only way that you know how to live. That event, that time, those people, and that place are the props to lack. When you remove from lack the association that keeps it propped up and you remove those props of association, there is no crystal ball. There was only the association. Lack doesn't even exist. It is incapable of existing in a kingdom of absolute abundance.

Do you know why you are insecure? Because someone — whoever you want to name — told you and made you feel insecure. And you keep going back to that time; you keep hurting over it. If we just looked at insecurity without the prop, there wouldn't be anything called insecurity, and what exists in the no-space is love. What is love? Love is the glue that holds everything together. Now that is the power.

CHAPTER 2
THE ART OF DETACHMENT
AND UNCONDITIONAL LOVE

*"All of these blocks are really empty and the only
thing that is real about them is blame. And when
we get rid of that, there is nothing else and all that
exists is love. That is the God quality that we are
after here. That is the power that moves mountains."*
— *Ramtha*

Unconditional love resides in the bosom of the Goddess. Why do I find that most beautiful of all? Because that means that woman has more love than association, and in the place of association nothing but love lives because that is what you have left when you remove the props of victimization in every level of your life. And I say that the Goddess is alive and well because from her bosom flows nothing but love. It is not contrived; it just is, because there is nothing else there except love. Why is that so important? Because that is the quality that makes a Christ. That is the love that heals, the love that binds, the love that sustains, and love cannot exist in a state of attachment.

One of the reasons that you keep this demon intact is because if you neutralized the shadow self within you, you are afraid of what you would be without it. In other words, what would be the stimulus behind your conversation? You are also afraid that you wouldn't have a reason to get up every morning and with blood, sweat, and tears make it through the day without having a nervous breakdown. Think of it. People are afraid to become naked to the extent of detachment, because what it means is there is real fear of what they may be or what they may become because they have shared a true and fruitful companionship with that which is termed the shadow self. They are attached to the attachments. That is an unnerving concept. Without going any further with this one-sided dialogue than this one statement — because I don't want you to create an attachment to the teaching that I just taught you, which is always a risk — just think that maybe the reason you are not willing to give up your past is because it has been such a companion in your present. It would really mean having to be a different person and, being the person who always wants to be in control of your attachments, then that puts you a little out of control. I tell you, saints are born out of this fire — they really are — and so are masters, true, genuine people who are on a divine mission to find that one flaw that has inhibited their progress for millennia. They are really after it. They really want it.

You don't have a whole bunch of karma. What you have is a flaw — a flaw — that can be owned, and it is the most obvious flaw in your life. It can be owned when you take a broadsword and knock the crutches out from under it and you find it is empty. It is the crutches that keep bringing you back lifetime, after lifetime, after lifetime.

We know in addressing such a teaching that there are those of you who don't hear me. You have what we call selective hearing and skip a lot. There are whole spaces of nothing remembered, and I am a much better orator than that. The selective hearing comes when you don't want to hear what I am telling you, but I tell you, you are here to hear it. You came here to hear what you did not want to hear before.

Our first step in this resolution is that it has taken all of these years to get you to a point of knowledge beyond superstition and beyond fanaticism, to get you to a point that we can move into the center and address this without hysteria. I am still going to have hysterical people because they don't listen. They don't hear the entire teaching, contemplate it thoroughly, and see for themselves that all of these blocks are really empty and the only thing that is real about them is blame. And when we get rid of that, there is nothing else and all that exists is love. That is the God quality that we are after here. That is the power that moves mountains. It took all of this time to get you to this little place to listen to this simple message, and it is that simple.

How hard is it then to become detached from your attachment? It is not hard at all, because with applied focus to your lack without people, places, times and events it cannot be sustained as lack; it doesn't exist. And when that enlightenment occurs, the brain will scramble to reconnect its circuitry to exactly that understanding. What happens when you realize there is no such thing in you as lack or fear or illness or evil or ignorance, or whatever else you want to say? What happens to you when you know that in that moment? The whole space of that contemplation is washed because it cannot sustain itself. It is washed and a power moves into it. It is free-space power; it is love. It is in that place that the miraculous takes place. The miraculous does not take place in the past and it does not take place in the future. It takes place in the moment you are present, in contemplation. That is when the miracle happens. That is the only space in which it can happen. What is the miracle? The miracle is abolishing the lie and in its place the abundance appears. It was always there. It has always been there.

Those of you who don't hear very well, you will continue to guard your dirty, little consciousness and your dirty, little thinking and be the possessors of your past because it gives you a reason to complain and a thing to work for, because you don't believe in me but you do believe in your lack. Those of you who hold onto your torment — your imagined torment, your imagined betrayal, your imagined nastiness of reaction — those of you who will hold onto it, your life will be nothing but hell not only the rest of this lifetime but all lifetimes to come. What is the payment of wages for being attached to this shadow self? It is that the love of this erroneous being becomes more seductive than the love for life. Its opportunities afford us every single day that the love of this beast is more important than the love of life, and by participating in that love — in every way, in every action, and in every thought — we could say that we are truly alive and indeed that we have truly lived. But your erroneous, little thinking will never allow you to experience life, and woe to you.

You will never be a master in this school because the wages of mastership are very strict. It demands self-conquest; moreover, it demands the absolution of the divine in us, which means the freedom of our divinity. And where is that divinity? It is right in the place that you think your lack is. And our divinity is the will. It is the sword of the will that allows us as lawgivers to determine what kind of life we want and to say there is no enemy, there is no man or woman or any parent that is so great as to rob me of my life and my power to make my life what I wish. No one was ever that great in my life, so why should it be in yours?

Those of you who have ears, listen to what I have said and interpret it no differently than the way that I have taught you. Those of you who want to know, your freedom is at hand. Your absolute lightness of being is at hand. I don't care who you are — I don't care what language you speak and if you can read or if you can write or if you can't — we are all equal in God. When we all have that moment to look at ourselves right in the eye, look at our limitations, qualify our lack by what sustains it and then remove what sustains it, then I swear we are enacting the divine and we all have the capacity to do that. Love is a magnet. It is magnetic and powerful. Lack is contrived, limited, destructive. Now the truly marvelous in this school is yet to be learned, but it cannot be learned until this lesson is practiced and owned.

Our first step to engaging this began prior to this lifetime, and it was our meeting this life — between you and I — and this school. That was the first step, that you asked and demanded the soul require of you in this lifetime a meaningful solution to your dilemma, to that one little problem. And when we satisfy the soul, then we are free to go on our way. I have now satisfied the soul by giving the conscious carrier of it the information that it needs to make decisions about that one little attitude and how to eliminate it. I cannot eliminate it for you — it is not my journey — but I am your Teacher and I can tell you this is the most rapid, the most volatile discipline you can do. It will thrust you into free space faster than anything I have taught you thus far, and it is a step that is ready for those who are willing to take it.

It doesn't sound like a lot but I promise you that letting go of your pride is indeed very hard to do. Being humble is very difficult for men and women to do. The act of forgiveness and the prostration of self in the act of forgiveness — prostrating means lying face down, spread like an eagle on the floor at the mercy of something greater — to prostrate yourself to something greater, that is the image we must do. What that means is that we are willing to give up what we are for something greater and to sacrifice it. It is not easy, but then again it is.

You are going to find that the moment you focus on that little problem or that attitude — and I forbade you to connect it with the past in any way, with a person in any way, with an event in any form, and I forbade you to connect it in time — and if under that direction you focus on that little attitude, you will find it will be nothing. Now you are learning the secret. All we have to do is first know the knowledge, and now you know the knowledge. The second thing you must do is to be willing to do it. And when do you do it? When do you want to: tonight, tomorrow morning, tomorrow afternoon? You choose. You just find it in yourself and I promise you, with a little help from your friend, it will surface. And when it does, you have as always the election to do something about it or let it ride. If you become decisive and do something about it, all you have to do is go someplace, close those eyes — blindfold them if you can — get into a place of quiet, put that blue star on, roll those eyes up, tighten down, and blow with the power breath of

Consciousness & Energy® and start moving energy.[4] And when you are ready, then you take that little attitude and you put it right in your focus without any other attachment. When you hold it there for a period of time, it is going to try to be slippery, and you are going to have to blow and bring it back into focus without attachment. The moment you do that, I promise you your world is going to change — your life, your flow of energy, and your freedom — and the next time that we are together, you are going to be older and wiser.

Everyone has asked the proverbial question throughout the ages: Master, what is unconditional love? Unconditional love is that which always is, and when attachment is removed, it is most brilliantly seen. It is not something you have to be; it is what you already are. In its place are supported illusions and lies, and when they are removed, the love is there. It does not have to be worked on. That is the nature of our beings, my beloved people. We were conceived in it; thus we are in it. Point Zero is it, and all the power that formed all of the dimensions and all the planes and all the heavens is that very power. And thus if we are conceived in the womb of such love, then that must be the aspect of our true nature. Being anything other than that is being artificial to that nature, and that is why we have what we call the wheel of reincarnation.

It Is Possible to Own It All in One Lifetime

Is it possible to own all of this in one lifetime? It absolutely is, because if one has the privilege of moving through life as a conqueror in conquering oneself, conquering the limitations

---

4 Ramtha's discipline of Consciousness & Energy® (C&E®). See the Glossary.

and its own ignorance, then one moves to that area naturally. Hopefully one is endowed with enough wisdom to see the wisdom and logic in dispersing of attachments, because in its dispersal there is no threat and there is no coloration of the self, so there is no little attitude that would bind one to another life.

Is it possible in one lifetime to drink in all the mornings that Ra rises and blisters the night sky with the color pink and rose and purple and red? Absolutely. And in one lifetime can you drink in that which is termed the waxing and waning of the moon till dawn? Is it possible in one lifetime to own the experience, that the experience is always? It absolutely is. And isn't it possible in one lifetime to have eaten and reveled in the food? Is it possible in one lifetime to have drunk enough wine? It absolutely is. Is it possible in one lifetime to have grown to such an extent that not even life itself is an attachment? It absolutely is.

I would never have wanted to be on the wheel of reincarnation because the wheel then would have been my enslaver. The most frightening and horrific thing that has ever happened to you is being born with no memory of who you once were. That is the wine of such enchantment that it is a terror. It is unthinkable not to be in full faculty of what I once saw and knew and experienced and to have it abolished from me for the sake of taking on a new child in a new body that cannot remember because the brain itself did not live in those times. To have had a brain that could not remember the mornings that I saw, indeed the evenings that I knew, the battles that I was in and the soldiers I interacted with, the smell of stench and blood and carnage — and, yes, jasmine and olives and the color of silver-leafed trees at green-reed rivers and wildfowl so brilliant and beautiful — the very thought of having that abolished from my consciousness is unthinkable. And yet I have watched you so many lifetimes starting over. To me, that is unthinkable. To you, you have never thought about it, which is the most horrible thing. You really are lost unless you have some way — some lantern that in the night of your ignorance and your lack of neuromemory can light a path for you — that you instinctually know to follow but cannot reason with your current brain why you should. What an imprisonment, and it is not easy to come out of it.

It is possible to do all of this in one life. And it is possible to teach your children to do it all in one life when you are wise enough to understand the traps that you walked into and to teach your children to walk into them and to get out of them. When you teach them that, you have given them life-giving, spiritual knowledge that will save them in the long run from having to live a life and wonder what it was all about, only to die, go back, and realize that one little issue you did not take care of this time. With this knowledge you cannot help but address the issue because it is the very thing that torments you. It is the thorn in your side and you know it very well. All you have to do is look at it.

In the days that follow from this, what I will do for you and what I can do for you is to raise your awareness of those little attitudes and I will help create circumstances around them so that you get to see them starting to bloom. And they are not bad and they are not good; they are opportunities. When you see the opportunity, understand I am pressing it to you to do something with it. You can do anything you want to do with it or you can go back to your old philosophy, your old horoscopes, your old drugs, your drinking out of control — you can go back to all of that — but you will never find resolve with it. That is your choice. Or instead you can become naked, unattached, and utterly and remarkably powerful. I know the way home. You are not going to get too out of control, I promise you. So be it.

Ramtha's Learning to Detach from His Physical Body

Student: I would like to know when you were practicing going in and out of your body, how did you know where you were? And did you go to other levels, like the fourth, fifth, sixth, and seventh? And if you did, were you taught there? And when you ascended in front of us, did you know where you were going? And if you had a life review — I know you weren't stripped — did you still have to look at your life and then go where you decided you wanted to go? I always wanted to ask you that.

Ramtha: The first time that I left my body, it was an accident. You remember the story of the wind? The reason that I knew that I left my body was because I found myself in an atmosphere of height in which I was unaccustomed to being. Moreover, having the point of view of which I could see my body — and there was no sensation in leaving it — the only awareness that happened was being above it, which is the usual case in leaving one's body.

Now being separated from my carnal self — though I had separated many from their carnal selves — I had never been separated from my carnal self, so it was a new experience for me. When I recognized my body and my robe and my plateau is the moment when I claimed the body as my own, and that was the moment I was brought back into it. Consciousness and energy creates reality.

Then for seven years I went out and reenacted everything — I am a patient God — for seven years. Where else was I going to go? For seven years I went out and I thought and plotted and planned, and I wondered and indeed pondered. What I did was build up an expectation, which can go nicely back with the teaching tonight. I put an attachment on an event that had no attachment. So we could say then that I built up a religious dogma about the event in analyzing it intellectually. That intellectual analysis is what prevented me for seven years from doing the same, marvelous thing again. When I gave up the expectation, then I gave up the attachment of my intellectual perception of it and that freed myself to move again.

The next time that I moved — which was seven years and a few days later — I moved to a point near the same point of distance from my whole awareness and my body. And the moment I knew that was my body again was the moment that I went back into it. I am very smart. I understand that every time I keep looking at this body and calling it mine is the moment I am back in my body. So some wonderful lessons followed subsequent to that. I had come to the place of surrender where I could leave. I knew I was gone because in various places that I left — most of which were my little hovel — I always got the viewpoint of the higher perspective observing a lower perspective. Coming back into my body was the recognition that it was my body, so after a while — and a while to me could be months and years — I understood that I needed a reference point to understand my detachment. But the moment that I recognized from where I came, I was back into it. So then the next step to the freedom was to no longer recognize my body and to no longer think about it. That took some mastery. The first years in this art I was not a traveler in dimensions and domains. I was an entity that was remote from my body and endeavoring to learn the process so that I could do it very well.

When I entered into the tunnel, or the ladder of Jacob, I did not go into dimensions and planes unknown to me. You understand, as I have taught you, that we all came down those stairs and from those levels, and the moment we reenter them we are clothed in the garment of that plane. When I left my body and entered into infrared, I put on the body of infrared. When I left my body and entered into light, I understood the light because I was there. My election to return to my body allowed me to return to my body fully cognizant of what the light meant and what I saw there. What I knew at the light was that there were preceding kingdoms. So the next time I visited the light I went beyond it, and in that I was clothed in the body of Shiva. Now if I then inhabit the body of Shiva, it is the body that I once knew. It still lives. And contained therein is all the knowledge that is afforded to me of a mind that lives on the fourth level, so I know where I am. Do you understand?

Student: Yes.

Ramtha: Now let me continue. It took me until the day that I left this plane to explore all of those planes and to wear all those bodies. And every time that I came back to the body, I brought with me all of that knowledge. I didn't leave it. I carried it back with me and brought it back to my physical incarnation. That meant then that I switched, as it were, as Ramtha from a yellow-brain or neocortex perspective. I became Ramtha from the deeper-brain perspective because only in the deeper brain did I seed the memory and carefully implement it into the yellow brain, into the neocortex.

When I ascended and left this plane, I did so because I had visited every other plane. In one nightfall here on Terra I would leave my body, and in time of another place — for example, on the fifth plane — in what was a nightfall here I lived for hundreds of years there and brought back the richness of that time frame by morning when my physical body awakened.

So to ask me did I gain knowledge and know where I was

is an understatement. By the time I left this plane, I communed with my people the simplicity of my teachings and my truth that I knew and brought it forward to them in simplistic style so that they would never forget me and understand how to live a life — a meaningful life — and that the kingdom of heaven held within its boundaries an unlimited opportunity for anyone on this plane to be a part of it. But the passion has to be there. The dedication and the patience have to be there. That I left and did not die in their midst was an unforgettable incident. The day that I ascended, I took my body upright and put its old robe on and walked it out in the middle of my people. And in the midst of my body I brought forward my seventh-level mind, and that mind vibrated this body into kingdom come.

The Egyptian Book of the Dead

Student: My father passed away last year in April and I was here for an event. My family lives in India and I heard about it at a friend's house, and when I heard about it, I sort of became numb but I didn't become emotional.

This was an evening event that we were allowed to come, and this was in the morning that I heard, the first day. I went into focus and I felt that I almost went — it was an immediate feeling — where I was in the room in his bedroom, and his body was lying there and I saw him in the corner. And when I saw him, he was really afraid. These are just my feelings. I have judged them afterwards as just being mere fantasies or something like that, but I am going to go on anyway.

When I saw him I said, "Why don't you come back with me?" And I felt that he came back with me. I don't remember the focus session after that. But what happened was that for about three days through the event I felt his presence on and off, that he was with me. Even when I was driving or whatever, I was aware of his presence.

In all those times I would go in and out of focus. And what I did was I talked to him, and I was trying to tell him everything that I couldn't share with him when he was in his body — whatever I had thought that I had learned, whether I knew it as a truth or as just mere knowledge — to share it with him because I felt that if he could benefit from it and go beyond to ultraviolet through me, or at least know about it, maybe in the next lifetime it would benefit him.

In the end what I had done was I felt that I was making a tunnel for him through the light in ultraviolet, and I created these blue webs, a tunnel of webs. And I told him that I would keep it open as long as I could so he could go through and see what the other side looked like and if he wanted to, he could stay there. But I felt in my mind there was a resistance and a distrust on his part, that he really didn't trust me because he didn't know. In his consciousness he had never been exposed to something like that. Even though he didn't have his present brain, the consciousness — the mind that he was occupying — did have the concept of ultraviolet, so I am not sure if he could go through.

My question is: Can you do that for another person, even if they weren't exposed to the teachings, for your family or your loved ones or your friends?

Ramtha: Have you ever heard of a book called *The Egyptian Book of the Dead?*

Student: No.

Ramtha: I will send you a runner. It is about saying the prayers of direction for the deceased and, in particular, the deceased in elder times were the greatest entities of the dynasties of Egypt at that time. It was the sacred prayers of directing the Spirit through the passages of infrared on to the light. Now that was a science brought forward to this planet by the Gods who understood the science. So obviously there is, in what you were able to do for your father, a revelation.

When you are out of the body, what you see is perceived with greater illumination and clarity than the body could ever offer. The perception of the Spirit in an ultrafine, subtle body is much more dynamic than it is in the human body. When the human body — as an instrument operated by the spiritual self — endeavors to make contact and its instructions can be received by the spiritual incarnate entity who is now discarnate, who is now in Spirit, this can provide an enormous pathway, a passage, if you will, to the other side and should never be neglected.

Yes, it worked, but the resistance that you felt was not from your father; it was from you because you didn't believe in what you were doing.

Student: Was it because I thought I was unworthy of doing that, that I wasn't knowledgeable enough, or just simple disbelief?

Ramtha: You just didn't trust what you already knew to be substantial enough to make a difference.

Student: Okay. Thank you.

Ramtha: Don't do that.

The Importance of Change for the Soul's Journey

Change is not a disease and it is not a virus. It is necessary for a person to continue to grow and to expand that growth in one's life, to have an effect upon life. It is important for the soul that we change, and the more that we do so in one lifetime, the greater our chances are of succeeding this lifetime, not with another lifetime but an onward journey back through the ladder, back to Point Zero. We enhance our opportunity of doing that. Now there are many of you forcing change in your life in areas that you are not mature enough to change. When I speak of a level of maturity, I mean that you have created circumstances in your life that you intentionally created and that you are in the midst of experiencing those creations.

There is no timeline to an intentionally created experience. For example, you may be in a relationship that has not reached a level of maturity to the point that the relationship no longer offers you the challenge by which to grow, and the challenge could simply be a matter of having the ability to respond in love. And if that is not there any longer, then that relationship has reached a maturity and it is time to change the relationship. Some of you will not find that level of maturity for years.

When I tell you to change, that does not mean that you are to get rid of what is in your life that you have not yet owned. It is easy to know and simple to know when you have owned something. It becomes boring, predictable, and tedious. And the rewards are as little as having a roof over your head and food in your mouth, and that is the compromise. It is simple to know and easy to detect when it is time to move on. Boredom is the sign that it is time to change.

Many of you are not finished with your experiences and have no business trying to change them when they are not mature. When they are mature is when you have reaped from them everything that you are supposed to reap from that which you intentionally created. You don't want to — and it would merely be impossible to — move out of love and cast it aside in favor of something bigger and better, because when love is present, that is never boring. That is ongoing and nurturing.

I want you to understand that the prerequisite to being a master does not mean that you have to vacate your life completely of everything in it because you think that means detachment. You only detach yourself from your suffering, your lack, and your victimization. You enjoy, by God, the fruits of your focused enterprise into life, and it is your job to experience it to the level of maturity. And when that maturity is reached, it will give you up; you won't have to do anything. It will give you up because there is no longer the magnetism or the dynamics involved in the continuation of it.

Do not make posthaste to destroy or try to destroy what is real in your life because you have misread the teachings. There is a time to enjoy what you have done, and that is the beauty of the master in life. But the master in life can come down from the mountain and enjoy the feast upon the once-empty table that he or she, the master, intentionally created and can actually sit down and partake of it. There is a time to stop visualizing and start eating or drinking.

There are days you are not going to want to do your focus, and why would you not want to do your focus? Because perhaps the only thing that you need to do when you wake up is to thank God that your eyes have opened to a glorious morn and that what you have already focused into your life is in full bloom. And you say, "God, give me the broadness of mind and the passionate aspect of character to absolutely enjoy it." Then the discipline is the life, the day that is well-lived. There are days that it is time to go back up on the mountain and go back to work and start changing the view down below. And then there will be a time to come down and enjoy it.

Yes, it is important that you change. You should not be the same person sitting here tonight as you were the first time you came to see me. If you are, we have a problem. Your life should be like a dancing star flashing in who knows what beautiful direction, and how long will the spike be and what coloration will it be. You should be changing and improving your state of mind, improving and sharpening your ability to find that center without pause, to reflect about any past circumstance that would deny you the richness of not having a problem. You should work on polishing yourself, and every day polish and take responsibility for your actions and don't put it off on anyone else. When you can no longer find the attachment to support the action, it will disappear out of your life and so will its effect in your life disappear.

There really is an extraordinary self inside of you that in the normal course of evolution would take many more lifetimes to cultivate because it is just being hung-up on one little issue of suffering. We know that it is that easy to kick the legs out from under its suffering and get rid of its associations and past. When we know it is that simple, then it is no longer in our life. And when we are bold enough to do that, we deserve to be that radiant being that is no longer affected by things from the past, people from the past, and no longer suffers under those criteria. We deserve to be radiant beings and indeed we deserve to be powerful in that radiant self. It is only those people that really do deserve the honor of living for two hundred or more years. They are not gauged to die anytime soon because they haven't suffered enough to destroy their own life force. Polish yourself. When you start whining, take a look at why you are doing it, at its heart, and get clean. It doesn't take a great deal of effort. Then you will understand the magical science of mastery and its effect called longevity.

And, last, it is true that before you were born in this life you knew about me, for I certainly have known you, and you made your way here and that was preordained before birth. This school had to come into being to facilitate those whose soul's choice was to find the knowledge that was at the root of the cause of their problematic behavior that kept binding them back into lifetime, after lifetime, after lifetime. And that knowledge has been addressed in this school.

We have fulfilled a destiny, you and I, on a soul level of providing the information and inspiring you to do something about it. I am heavy in that department. But unless you want to do it, it will never work for you. I promise you that after this life, those of you who don't apply the knowledge are going to find yourself back up there in another life review, and you are going to look at your silly antics of choosing to hold onto a rather sour attitude that is really despicable and dishonorable. You would rather hold onto that than release it so you can be free in lifetimes to come. You are going to look at that and you are going to be sad beyond belief at your pride and indignation in holding onto it. After you address this little attitude, there is much I can show you and indeed much we can do. But not until you come into the center where I live can I show you around adequately. So be it.

I didn't come to just give you a brilliant teaching, which of course I did do. But I also, as the Lord of the Wind, speak as a lawgiver, that all I should say and all that I should answer should carry the power of full manifestation, and that I did tonight. What this means to you is what I have taught you will manifest in your life and the opportunities will come to you in glorious measure. I want you to have a chance to see what I was endeavoring to show you tonight and indeed give your soul a chance to have a reprieve. With the words comes the power. So be it.

I love you. That is all. So be it.

Chapter 3
The Last Battle against Tyranny and Slavery

> *"You came here in the midst of conscious collapse.
> It is when the programming of the personality is so
> intact and so ingrained that right and wrong is the
> nurture of your daily bread: to do right because you
> are so wrong, to form identities that are alien to
> the greater thought."*
>
> — *Ramtha*

The Conquest of Our Personal Limitations

O my beloved God,
this day I have grown.
This day I am unfolding.
Change, my beloved God,
hath been a bitter fruit.
O my beloved God,
alas, it was only my fear.
Unfold me, troubadour,
unfold me.
Give me the strength
to understand
and the wisdom to choose.
So say I
from the Lord God of my being,
forever
and ever
and ever.
So be it.
To life.

It has taken a very long time in your time — from the few seeds of entities who came in the very beginning to audience — to gather unto this great place your wonderful number. It is a tribute to the possibility that God is personalized, individualized, and indeed unified. It is a tribute to truth. It has taken many arduous moments and difficult words in a meaningless language to bring you even here this evening in your time and counting. But I stand, as it were, in a body not of my kind to greet you, to deeply salute you for your courage as children to have come this far from such meager beginnings in this time frame.

This body is indeed unto me an august body, a potentially royal body, a body that can challenge limitation but, alas, only when it has challenged its own personal limitation. The blight of any one entity's growth has never been the lethargy of Spirit being weak and the body weak but the insistence upon right and wrong and being caught in such a trap.

To think differently is an alien prospect in the entity, but to think differently is to have the reward of an unlimited experience that lifts you up from the turbulence and the trap into a thoughtfulness of being that indeed allows the evolution: the wings to grow, the Spirit to grow, the body to fly. Children only imagine such wonders. So how long has it taken you to come here? The greatness in which I salute all of you is your tenacity and indeed its small voice that rings beyond that which is termed the rights and wrongs and the thinking in this world that compels you to know — as one would put it in a more primitive aspect — to seek, to find, to realize. There has been a language barrier between us, but that is all that was ever between us. I am most pleased in you.

It is going to get very rough and very difficult, but like any children with an astute parent — wise, dignified, noble, and profoundly loving — the child will grow, will grow not only in body but a mind proportionate to meaningfulness, purpose, to morals that supersede mediocrity that go to the sublime. The child can grow in the subtleness of understanding and never be hindered by fear or threats but be righteously compelled on its journey. That is where you are, children learning righteousness, and I am pleased you are home tonight to understand more.

In my lifetime, war was not a known science. Squabbling, sibling rivalry, and neighborhood jealousies all existed. Tyranny and slavery were the order of the times, and so little has changed from that time. Because of my intense drive and intent will to do whatever I set my mind to do, that developed in me the proponents that would allow a collapsing of the old and a building of the new. My life speaks of that very well.

In my ignorance of freeing people from my enemies — anyone was my enemy that wasn't on my side in the beginning — it was clearly defined: the law was the sword and that was all there was to it. There was no back talk; hence the term "clear-cut." I have always appreciated a no-nonsense approach to decision-making. And yet as a man grows up to be a man very early and goes through the battles of his body, the battles of his mind, the battles of his Spirit/consciousness — and then, of course, the opposing battles that are so real, the enemy — I changed a great deal. Hormones helped, being ignorant helped, and being fearless was the greatest help of all. But I changed. I conquered. I did what I did and thought that I had done away with the people of the three Gods but, to my disgust, what replaced them were the ministries of worship, another form of tyranny.

I also would realize in the latter part of my life that something had to be done about this forever and ever and ever, something real. Once you are a strategist and a warrior — and you bear the ever-painful wounds and memories, you understand the difference between the smelling of fresh blood and rotting blood — your consciousness forever after is always molded in making life better, doing away with ignorance, superstition, and unworthiness, great factors. I understood that as long as humanity remained slaves — no better than the dog in the street or the trash from the marketplace — as long as humanity had that consciousness, they were doomed forever and ever and ever because in the wake of my march, worship became the king, worshiping an empty idolism. And speaking on my behalf, no one speaks on my behalf. Perhaps you understand why, and you understand why even this hour there is none other like me worthy to hold my name, to interpret my words, to excuse my behavior, for in my life, in the wake, such caved.

Vision of the Collapse of Human Consciousness

As a warrior who was fine-tuned and addressed to this sort of life who was converted to a greater consciousness, I had great vision into the future. I made it my business. I always had great vision. Fearlessness does that to you. Leading people, being the head of your family, being a father or mother develops that in you. I was the father of over two million people, and growing. I was their father.

In those times, before the vapors of this crustacean of physical form left this place, I knew where I was going and what I would dissolve into. But before I left, I also knew in my day generations yet unborn, the recycling of yet unborn people, and where at any point in history that would change.

You cannot dispose of or rebuke human will. And if they don't have it, then you stand in on their behalf. That is the basis of government. That is the basis of the priesthood and of all entities that speak on behalf of God and speak on behalf of the people. You will never, ever understand human will until you have earned the right to possess it. It does not come easily. Do not confuse stubbornness, hate and joy, acceptance and denial for will. Those are primitive actions that eventually lead to will. When you understand will, you will understand what I am telling you. It is my great desire that this freshening aspect, hereto unrealized, be more closely defined in the coming days in school, that you understand what it is and have the opportunity to possess it. It is the difference between being children and adults. It is the difference between mortal human beings and Gods immortal. When you understand, you see that this is one precious opportunity in the cycles of this plane of demonstration that cannot be erased and washed away, that it must be remembered at least every fourth generation. It must be ingrained creedlike, if necessary.

I was then and there looking upon this form of life and seeing far, far, even to this very night. Who is to say that me speaking to you now are not my thoughts this very night so long ago. Perhaps it is, in a hovel on the side of a great mountain. It was implemented and willed that there would come from nowhere extraordinary human beings — extraordinary, simple and extraordinary. They would become the golden threads in the tapestry of this evolution that would glisten and never fade — when all the colors of every kingdom that come and passeth can fade in their beauty — that the golden thread remains untarnished, brilliant, to the very end. And thus it was set out in great certainty that entities were sent into the world, great beings — not stubborn beings, not liars, cheats, pretenders, not scholastically intelligent, not beings who think they have been chosen, but a rare consciousness. So noble was their purpose that they would always rally at very critical points in human history, a small group of people, to carry on the concept that divinity is the divine right of every human being. Every human being is only defined that they are from the loin and the fruit of the womb, that they possess a body of flesh and blood and sinew and tears and hair and youth and age. That is a human being, but a God can exist as a human being. These Gods were great teachers that were sent out at critical times of conscious collapse.

What brings on conscious collapse? You came here in the midst of conscious collapse. It is when the programming of the personality is so intact and so ingrained that right and wrong is the nurture of your daily bread: to do right because you are so wrong, to form identities that are alien to the greater thought. The consciousness is collapsing. No one knows who they are except what they can tell you they are through family tradition, their pains and their scars of growing up, their successes and failures. Every one of you has them and that has been your identity. That is the sign of social consciousness, and it is collapsing to such a degree that your next generation could not fathom personal choice, the greater thought. The great schools were developed on this concept.

Who thinks of such a concept? What sort of being with far vision would make certain and put into place the prospect of salvation, not from a Christ but from knowledge rich in experience with the beginning words, "Know that you are God. You are greatly loved." It doesn't mean anything but it is a beginning. The schools flourished, knowledge flourished. It was spoken openly because honor was learned prior to knowledge coming openly.

Do you know what honor is, to be rich in honor, impeccability, to take in and not to let out but to hold an experience upon it? Few of you knew that; few of you yet have learned it. Then the knowledge came — it was free — of who you are, where you came from, the ability to see backwards, to see all that in the great consciousness of the mind, to be able to lay the king's table out in front of them, a bounty that seems to come from everlastingness, stretching all the way to eternalness, and saying to them, my beloved, this is your destiny. You have walked through the light. You now belong to the ages of time. You are here to learn all of the following things: You are a spaceship in mass. You are an explorer. You are a creator, and your species will flourish. But do not flourish your species — do not give birth — until you have seen all there is to see here, until you have drunk wisdom from this cup of virtue, an ennobling wine that is intoxicating that takes you to immortality. Then lie with the man, lie with the woman, bring forth the fruit of the womb, for then you will be responsible enough to bring in a God, responsible enough to rear it and one day show it its potentials.

These people learned, had the patience to learn. Though they belonged to the ages, they were trapped in time. Their Spirit was free but their body was slow. They could cast their mind on yonder hill and describe a freshening brook and green reeds, a beautiful woman with alabaster knees and green eyes, and suddenly the body lurched to go beyond the hill. The mystery was if you knew that, why weren't you there? It became obvious that the entrapment to the ages was mass, the physical plane of acceptance. The physical plane has its laws, its dictates that say in order to enjoin the beauty that lies beyond the hill near the brook of green reeds, you must get up and run across the desert, and may the Gods put wings on your feet to carry you nigh to your lover's waiting nest.

Why was that necessary? Isn't it obvious? If you knew what was beyond the hill, why can't you instantaneously be there? You were, you are, but you belong to the ages. You are now in the midst and the control of mass that can be seen as a detriment or yet a great advantage. The fool condemns his body, takes his life, locks himself in a prison, despises what he is. The wise one says, alas, to be this, to be the man of virile loins, to be this with a heart that beats like a great steed, to be this with the sweating of musk on a pounding temple — to be that, one and the same — that is the wise man. The students learned that. They learned all of the knowledge that you say you are ready to learn, but you are weak in learning it. Honor has not been established.

Strategy to Preserve the Truth of Our Divine Inheritance

The schools flourished and the golden threads of immortality were turned out and they disappeared. They vanished into the vapor of early morn, never to be chained or whipped or abused or identified. They live even this hour. They have never died; they have lived on. In every age they have perpetuated their great evolution because every age to which they belong they are eating of the table that was set in front of them, from everlastingness into eternity. In every age they are the quiet force that works on behalf of preserving knowledge, preserving truth, putting out a powerful, conscious call, supporting, so that the golden thread can produce another golden thread. It was a success, as I knew it would. Then the schools were infiltrated, and so they took the knowledge into symbolism, into dance. They took their teachings into stone and mortar, and the weak ones were destroyed, the fearful ones. So it has been.

Very, very few of these entities have any of you ever heard about. You wouldn't, really, because there are some of them that go by several names and perhaps one name got remembered. But who were they when that generation passed and the bones of children lay bleaching in the sands or were devoured by the worm? Who were they then? This has been critical. I always learned in my life and would desire it to be so that you be the same in that richness of learning. I gained the wisdom to understand that what was in front of me would be repeated after me.

This school exists this moment from the consciousness of the Ram contemplating this school this moment, contemplating the strategy of this moment in a very simple hovel while a fire rages on a hearth and Crosham blazes. And it is happening. It is happening then and it is happening now. So why me now? Because I have given runners in the past who would say this event would come and that it would be I. I have sent the vibration through the golden threads that this would occur.

Who would resonate to me? Those who are encamped outside that are contemplating a separateness of the Father from his children, for it is befitting that as grief and confusion set in on all my people, that my vision is turned far into generations untold. To find and mark a place in the Void, mark a place in the ages on the power of your grief 35,000 years ago — on the power of emotion — that riding upon that energy, the grief of those times would set a time that the Father return to his children, the warrior to his people, the man to his godhood.

This moment is a great moment stretching forth into time as one who begins to learn remote-view — twisting time backwards and forwards and seeing it in a virgin moment — not caught in the past or the future but the splendidness of Now. Now you grieve and now you are here simultaneously, and the power of that time has created me in this time. Why now? Why did the eyes of consciousness stop now? Because I am the last of the golden threads. I am the one who set them in motion tactically and strategically. That was my greatest experience, don't you know. With the wisdom of consciousness, I understood energy as a mandate, a manifestation of consciousness. I understood no-time — ascension time and time again — because Now is a point that you are referring to as critical mass.

War drums, human slaughter, the plagues, the One World Order, the marks of beasts, are here. And as always it only takes a few, as it always took a few, not the world. Everyone that is parlaying is parlaying on the heads of the world. The greed is the world. We don't need that; only a few.

Why does everyone say that they are the chosen ones? Why indeed does every religion say they are the chosen ones of God and everyone else is condemned into hellfire for all eternity? Why does every government suppose that it is the elite of the world? Why is it that neighbors think they are better than their neighbors? Why does "betterness" have to do with things? It has to do with attitudes. I am telling you the same thing. Are you chosen? I will tell you how you are chosen. You are here because I desire you to be here. But the desire — remembering, honoring will, even though you don't have it yet — is honoring that you are going to have it. The will is that some of you — or perhaps the majority of you — at this very moment many, many nights ago are in temporary quarters on the side of a great mountain. The night has a cold wind but the sky is clear. One moon is shining in its quarter; the other is setting. And I have people who know that I am leaving them who are emotionally grieved.

Such as for a splendid few of you if I were to tell you indeed this evening, "I shall come no more; remember me in your consciousness," I assure you there would be those of you in this audience that would grieve deeply because I would be greatly missed. I know that. You are the ones that I am talking about, and you are the ones who heard my name and came. That was the voice of remembrance. You don't set into all eternity a manifestation unless it is built on the truism of willful, powerful emotion. The greatest, emotional moment was this night so long ago. That is what set the memory of this most precarious, indeed, entity before you. That is why you are here. Something had to link you present-day, forgetful beings to something immemorial, something that reaches to the core of your being of remembrance, and it was grief. Otherwise, like all things that are beautiful, that are imitated and are made a mockery of, it would still have collapsed and fallen into the abyss.

There is a deep and profound binding, if you will, of you and me. For you it is an unexplainable, mixed feeling, one of confusion at many moments and at others profound admiration and deep love. And you know I am right. For me, you were worth your weeping women and soulful men, your campfires, holding onto the past, and the battle cries and all of those stories. For me, it was you, my beloved people, who I detested in the beginning and came to love with such a love that passeth all understanding. It went to eternity. Now it has come together.

I knew I would select a woman. I came to love them and respect them, understand their plight and their curse in the times to come, and understand their understated intelligence to use, as a tactician, their heightened, emotional energy as power. The greatest and noblest love was to select a woman in which this consciousness can resound over 35,000 years, and I selected well. You had best make your peace with this entity, for this entity is the hull of the ship that has its anchors in the sky — your jealousy, your hatred, your bitterness, your envy — for it may be the ship that takes you home or accounts for preservation. Wake up and understand how this is working.

Once I went into a great city — white marbled walls, beautiful. You could see them as you turned for kilometers, miles. Ruthless people lived there and beautiful people with such silken tents and awnings in the marketplace that would even bedazzle your spoiled eyes. I went invisible, undetectable. I went not in the brazen breastplate. I went not with the ring. I went not with the headband. I went disguised, invisible. A little big, but I was there. I got the job done. I am here disguised completely from even those who fear me because I would never stoop so low as to use such a vehicle. I have climbed high to use it and to find it, and I am getting the job done. But why I?

My business at this point is getting you beyond your human phase into that consciousness that is sublime and to the thought that is immortal, getting you beyond your pettiness that works so well for all your reasons why you should remain a slave. You are stupid and ignorant and all you think about is who you are going to lay tonight, how much you are going to guzzle tomorrow night, and how you look. Don't you know they know that? Don't be so small as to presume that in the eyes of coldness, liken unto steel, you are not worthy for consideration. Your actions have given you away.

At this time in my thought, upon the bittersweet reverie of grief, was to take you further than you have ever gone in the mind — beyond the myth, beyond hypnotism — to take you further than any human being in ages has gone into the developmental processes of consciousness everlasting. That is my business. I have legions doing other things. This is my business for the emotion out of which this moment was created.

Using Emotional Energy As a Tool for Change

You are here under a Master Teacher — and I am indeed that and more — with the gathering of a few great entities whose only reason for really being here is because something profoundly touched them. And for as many reasons as they have had to leave and to deny me — which is very obvious, I have set it up that way — they have with great tenacity stayed and clung. If that were the only reason, that mysterious, inner devotion — if that were the only reason, the hook, why you do any of this — then that was reason enough because in the spark of love, indeed in the spark of emotion, in the height of hate, the height of joy, compassion, the height of freedom, that is the moment long-awaited that one moves in that energy, but not until then.

If this mysterious devotion has been the reason for your discipline, for your hanging onto this school, the reason that you have moved here and changed, then you never had any other reason other than that to do it. You did not have the emotional wisdom to make that decision because everything I told you, the world denied. So it takes emotional energy. It takes learning how to build it and then use it at critical times to develop upon. In this moment of flickering fires — and the murmur on that cool breeze of an old man's rumbled words that sit here this night, mute — if the only reason you did all this is for this long-lived, unraped, unstripped devotion, then that was reason enough to come here to begin the processes, because fundamentally you had nothing else to come here on except grief. I am fulfilling a promise, not a verbal promise but a promise of profound love — an allegiance, as it were.

A greater-than-life being I am and was. I am here to use that to take you from whence I come, to teach you methodically, patiently — reiterating — working you until at some point you find another peak of emotional deliverance. The moment you do that, I will move you immediately into a new truth. I have business with you, and the business is to take a few — perhaps chosen by grief, deep emotion, transmuted into will — preserve you and teach you self-preservation wisely through all of the murk and the mire of what is really old news that is happening this hour, to preserve you from harm's way, not to send you into battle but to keep you tight, keep you marching, learning, and keep you focused.

I never had a city that could be attacked. My people — my women, my children, my old men and beloved old women — marched with me, and they were in the center of the most powerful army on foot that ever lived, for they were the prize.

Your business, upon my advice, is your choice — upon what I have told you nigh many days ago in your time and counting — to preserve yourselves. It is my business to get you over being slaves and mortals. And one day you survivors are going to see what has been teaching you. In some very thoughtful moments — for this too has been seen — you are going to truly wonder why I made it my business to handle you and your kind and to come to such levels of discussion and language. You are going to be in awe because, truly, the world is liken unto a speck of dust. And then you will understand, but you will ask yourselves why.

So am I this very moment sitting and watching the flames of a fire flicker on a great sword, shadows dance on the slanted roof, phantoms of the past? What are you doing this moment? Women, have you prepared your mead, served up the olives, the goat cheese, delicious bounty? And is the discussion this night in your camp a foreboding one? Are you weeping, because where is your leader going? Something is in the air. And, men, are you young or old? Are you out of your hovel because you do not want to show your sadness and your weakness to your family, to your woman, who knows it anyway? Are you sitting with the old guard? Are you reminiscing? Are you trying to outthink me again, which you never could do? Is it happening? Are you there and here? Can you smell it? Can you taste it? Remote-view; there is no time.

Where are the eyes, those great, black eyes? As they stare into the fire are they seeing your face now 35,000 years ago? Are they looking at this room? How does it appear? Does it appear

75

real or is it a dream? Are these eyes moving? Are they seeing from a distant past? What are they seeing? Do they recognize and understand what has been said? Do they understand their reaction?

Is it possible at this very moment there was never any history, there was only then and now? Is it possible that you never had a past? What were all those memories about your youth — do you remember? — your adulthood? What was all that pain about? Is it possible that in this moment you never had a past? Is it possible that you are there, wishing to be here? And if the past doesn't exist, who is to say that in your greatest moment of grief you have leaped forward to here to make it so? Is it possible? If it ever is, this will be the first and beginning instance of a revival of unspeakable knowledge.

What are all those memories? Are they like the phantoms on the fire that I see dancing across the wall? Is the glimmer and the fire that comes off of the great sword, is that the light? Are the memories just a flame flickering, casting a shadow? Are your memories shadows, and are you a fire? Is it possible you never have been anywhere other than there and here now? Because this very moment it is happening.

There are those of you who have turned off because what I am speaking is so bizarre — unearthly, edging on the absurd — that you haven't heard a word I have said. But those of you who have listened and are caught up in the emotional tide — that night that is happening now, that exists now as its transmuted form — will understand what dimensional mind is going to be all about. What I have just told you is the greatest puzzle of all. And if you can put it together, then my business here is indeed fruitful.

Where is yesterday? Are all those memories real? How real are they? Can you verify they are real? And how do you verify the verification? Could it be that all those memories were just thoughts contemplated upon and that Now is the mother of time? Could it be that yesterday never did exist, all those memories you have? I am talking about your life. What if it is a hoax? Only consciousness and energy — consciousness in its most primitive form of fear and grief and anxiety and love and joy — those are the pregnant moments that dictate time. Those are immortal. They are the strings of the fabric of this tapestry. They are not visual; they are a hunger deep inside.

There has been, in a greater understanding, no time expedited at the same moment I sit in my hovel to this moment. I hear the moaning, I smell the incense on the wind, the moon has waxed and waned.

You are here. You have the emotion. You have the memory. My business is with you. If you contemplate what I have told you this night from the most sincere parts of your being, perhaps a greater emotion will come up: one that is fortifying, something that you can spring from to manifest, something that gives a person self-determination. Without that in you, you will never figure out or completely understand the riddle I just gave you because you will still be a three-dimensional, captured, programmed human being that belongs to the ages and cannot fathom what I have said.

If you are determined to meet me in this moment of yesterday — and it is going to take as much effort on your part and nearly divine will — I will take you beyond this dimension in a study, a rigorous one, that will allow you the will to change your reality and effect personal destiny. You are going to have to get responsible and wake up and understand that time is running out on the commodities. Time is running out on the freedom to be able to place your home in the Earth, on the Earth, and one day above the Earth. You are going to have to take the responsibility to do it. Now if that seems a bit burdensome to you, then I suggest you go back to the world and its temporary convenience, because you do not have what it takes to come to the crest of where I left you 35,000 years ago on a mountain. You do not have what it takes to go up on that mountain.

I love you people with an encompassing passion. You are my people and I was and am your Ram. The moment came as I saw and see. Take my wisdom and apply it straightaway, for I tell you this for no other reason. One day the garb, the cloak, will come off from visiting this foreign time and, because you have chosen yourself through the emissary of passion, you will inherit this place quite different than what you see today. You will have the skills and consciousness to restore and to heal. Like the fish that live underground and the frog and the wasp and the ant, you will come alive one day and you will have an opportunity to fulfill a dream.

What is the dream? To have seen in your lifetime the washing away of inhumaneness, to see in your lifetime a small generation of people who think in like terms. All the machines will be turned off, so the freedom of thought will be an intoxicating beverage. The dream is to know what it is to live in paradise where there is no more disease that has been perpetrated upon the species, where there is no suppression, and you can heal with the power of a touch and resurrect a seed in the impregnated earth and make it into a tree in the twinkling of an eye. You are going to do that, but not until all of this is brought to its knees by its own hand and that which it worshiped will come back and reward it justly. And then a great legion will move into position.

In the meantime the dream will have been realized: peace on Earth and goodwill to men and women, joy and longevity of life, and primeval urges put away in the sinful closet and remembered as perhaps only the phantoms of a dream while sitting in front of a fire. So be it.

Now for the rest of this splendid evening — while the fires from the camp in the past slowly go out and burn into embers and there is a restless sleep among my people, and I never felt so grand — you take the emotion, if you have any, of what you have learned this night, take it to the Void. And what are you going to do there with it? Be it. It, through evolution, will present itself as opportunities. Those of you who want to move out of the ages into the beginning teaching of dimensional mind, I have certainly given you an opportunity in what are memories to move out of the ages and be something else. The most powerful moment in ever doing that is finding the height of emotion to do it.

If you dance to the rhythm of the music, then you have gone nowhere. If in flight and great passion, the music disconnects the frequency. First you are the music, then you begin to mutate into other lifeforms in consciousness. It is then that you have accomplished it. Engage in the dance of dimensional mind or go to the Void, but participate. You may sit here with your eyes blindfolded and contemplate all that I have said — for certainly I have said a lot, but not nearly enough — and as you do, let this thought come to you: Which eyes do you possess today, those of yesterday or the projection of yesterday to today? And was there ever really a past? Maybe it was all a lie, a hoax.

I love you. Your great tree sprang but from a few noble souls. Don't you know you are their fruit? The light is coming in the sky and the cookstoves are burning. It has been a wonderful night all across time. Love I you greatly. Do not go with a heavy heart but one filled with the potential of wisdom, and with that you can do great things. So be it.

Chapter 4
Redefining the Self As the Spiritual Self

*"We as consciousness and energy, the Godhead itself,
have only one real destiny — real destiny — and
that is to make known the unknown. The more that
we do so to imagine the unimaginable, the greater our
unity as God, as oneness, becomes. That is what we
are supposed to do. We are an ocean seeping into the
shores of the Void, and we should be expanding that
which we are. That is what the self is."*
— Ramtha

Abolition of the Self through Blame and Victimization

O my beloved God,
this night I am grateful
for my life
above all else.
Everything else
is illusion.
This life,
the blood
that pumps in my veins,
is you, my Holy Spirit,
and everything else
is illusion.
Of this night
I do celebrate
that which I am
as God manifest.
My beloved Father,
my beloved Mother,
of these days
lift me from my turbulence
and set me upon
the ground of your being.
So be it.
To life.

It is so beautiful to watch you and listen to your thoughts. We are going to talk about heaven, the Plane of Bliss. We are going to start this teaching by you understanding an important aspect of yourselves.

You wanted the spiritual journey in this life. You wanted it. You are here because I dreamed this time and all of you — even those of you who are not here, those that are gathered in other places — a gathering place, a time of maturity, given eons to play out the human experience. But aside from that, you also had to be ready. This is important for every individual in this audience to understand, because from that is a springboard to understand the rest of this teaching and to understand this school and your journey in it. Every decision starts with you. The ultimate reason for being here is I provided the hub and you came, but you had to be ready to come.

What I want you to understand is that everyone in this audience chose in this lifetime to evolve themselves spiritually. Now that is important because it empowers you to understand the meaning of this life and perhaps its journey and that the true destiny of life, and particularly this one, is not about what you accomplish; it is about becoming. That is what is important in this life.

There is no one here that should ever say that they are here against their will because that is not the way that it is set up. Everyone is here freely and engaging in the knowledge and its practices by choice.

The majority of the group chose to be here in this lifetime — as hard as that may be for some of you to swallow — because when you are here and it is going well, you are happy for the journey, but when you leave this and go out in the marketplace and put back on your fleshy body, you find a conflict between the ongoing, physical reality that you keep repeating and the spiritual reality that was really the destiny for being here. There is a gap in destiny and follow-through of that destiny in the human incarnation, but that has always been apparent.

Given that then, I want each of you to understand that somewhere you made a choice to be here and that you made a choice about really dedicating a life, a human life, a human incarnation, to the sole development of the spiritual self, and that is why you are here. If this was not your destiny, you wouldn't be here tonight, or you wouldn't be in this school, or you would be the gray, in-between entity who is not wholly present anytime they are here. They are only here because of someone else.

If in a state of human and spiritual maturity we can take and grasp this as a truth, then the truth empowers us. When we do not grasp this and are still wondering why we are here, we are not empowered by what we learn. We first must be empowered by recognizing that there is a self who is divine that can be empowered. That is why it is important for an entity to recognize their actions as their actions because it is always defining self and always empowering self.

Blame, as a side note, is a disingenuous quality of the spiritual person because blame then unempowers the self. When you blame someone else, you are draining the powerful resources of self. What happens is that self then starts to be hidden under that which is termed the fog of misunderstanding. Here in this school it is important that self always be the core, and power must always be generated from that core, and the power from that core at no time should be ever given away to someone else. Blame and victimization — those aspects of human characteristics — are the most important ingredients in removing the place of power from self and giving it away.

In order to fulfill this journey here, self must be defined. It must be defined not only as the spiritual self, but the spiritual self must be definable within the human self. All of this defining and polishing leads to the impeccable life, the empowered life.

If you chose this life for this spiritual journey, then that empowers you because it gives the place of destiny to you, and that is where it should belong. That is also consistent with you as a God having free will, the will that is free enough to imagine the unimaginable but the unimaginable springing from the core of self along with its power. If we abolish the self through blame and victimization and living in the past, we then unseat the very aspect of the spiritual journey. We disenthrone the God inside of us in favor of past incidents that we can blame our miserable, wretched, and failing existence upon. That is an undefined self, a power utterly given away, that when such a creature endeavors to manifest, there is no thrust from the core self in order to bring it forward. If no one is on the throne, the unimaginable cannot be imagined. Furthermore, there is no power to do it, to do anything with.

When I said from the first moment I appeared here that you are God, you are all God — forgotten, yes — it is my job to help you remember that. It is the nucleus of the spiritual journey. You chose to be a part of that journey, to define God — to define God and to seat that divinity within self — and when we do so, self becomes definable. Only when we have defined the self do we get to occupy it. It is only when we occupy it that we then become utterly empowered for the unimaginable. Up to that point it is not going to work, never will. Now this destiny, before you came into this life — and we are going to talk about the Plane of Bliss — was an option seen that all of you, except for a few, were ready to take on. We are going to understand that in a deeper aspect. At this particular point I want to say to you that unless self can be empowered fully, then the spiritual life — that which you came here to experience — will never be realized.

The walk of the master will never be walked by you until you leave no footprints in yesterday, because the past was the generation of growth that meant essentially the giving away of power to greater elements of authority. That authority could have simply been your classmates in the first grade, the beginning of what we call social consciousness, or giving your power away to your parents and the way that you were raised. That then starts the bleeding, if you will, of a life that is disjointed and seemingly has no purpose but to coast and ride and barely get by. It is a life that the unimaginable is not a part of but only what is in trend and what is easy.

In the spiritual walk of the master, we are going to have to manifest in your life what is called revelation so that it is revealed to you on each of your individual levels what the past and my term for it really means. We can never abolish the memories of who we were, but what we must do is transmute the energy of what we were, a disenthroned entity searching for self. We must take the energy that we have in the neuronet off of it and bring the power of that neuronet to continuously repeat day, after day, after day those circumstances of your past because it is hardwired in your brain. That hardwiring takes the power and distributes it to hold in place that which the past dictated. That is unacceptable for a student in the spiritual work because, number one, there is no spiritual work without power and, number two, there is no power without a sense of self. If self has not been reclaimed and redefined, then there is no such thing as the unimaginable, as man or woman being master of reality. It doesn't work; it hasn't worked. In understanding that — listen carefully — the past means to abolish victimization, abolish envy, jealousy, hatred, malice, to abolish that which is termed the aspects that are so degrading to the spiritual self that literally strip it of its beautiful power and hold together the demons of your own mind. The stripping of all of that means taking responsibility for those actions and making the responsibility one of self. When we do, then the blaming no longer is locked up in your pitiful parents — who, by the way, are spiritual people as well — or locked up in your first-grade class. It is no longer locked up in your need to be needed.

What happens when you say, "I created this — I cannot tell you why I created it or when I got the idea to create it, but I did it; otherwise it would never have occurred" — is you no longer have the outlet of continuous blame focused on entities or an entity in your life. Suddenly the cord is cut, the chains are cut, and the self begins to be defined.

The Dark Night of the Soul

When the self begins to be defined is a mournful moment because human beings by nature are cowards. They are cowards because they are afraid to be confronted by their own choices, so in a state of fear you run and point the finger at someone else. Pointing the finger at someone else is your cowardly way of excusing the circumstance. When you do that, when you point this finger of power, it means that this mind of power has focused the energy, reflected it back off of you to someone else, and thus you are dethroned. It is not a simple measure, I assure you, to take responsibility for your life, but it is the bravest, spiritual part in us that does, no matter how painful it may be. And what is the pain? The coming home of the prodigal son of energy.

We call this the dark night of the soul. All of that suffering is now full-bore upon us because it is energy returning to the Source. It is through the suffering that we are purified, because once the energy passes the barrier of the emotional body — and the emotional body is disturbed and ruffled, the heart beats fast and the breath is shortened, the tears begin to roll — that means the energy is coming back and it is causing a storm. You have to live in the storm. It is the nature of the child coming home. When the storm is over, energy now being purified through the emotional body has returned full cycle and its coming home is the necessary ingredient in defining the self, that which we are.

Now no one is ever going to make you take credit for your life. You can give lip service to this, but the true warrior is one who does it and does it very well — it is the conquest of self — and does it in a fashion knowing full well that what they have put out is coming back home manifold. It is the one who does this that in the end is liberated.

All beings who on Bliss chose the spiritual life know that in making such a choice it is not the easy path, that it is a path of defining the self and polishing it. They can't even imagine what that is going to mean in their life until they get into it. It is at this juncture that most people turn tail and run. Why? It is simple. Unless the divine that we are sits within the throne of this temporal body, it can never create the marvelous unless it has been divined and defined in ourselves. Unless that happens, the unimaginable is not going to happen to you, nor will that which is termed the righteous happen to you.

These measures of myth, dream, and legend always remain that to the chronic victim, and as they remain as such we marvel at those who seem to get through and do the miraculous. We are marveling at one who has passed the bridge, who has made the journey — the journey into recalling power back to self — and has lived through it. Those who cannot face it and are cowards and run from it are never again empowered with the lucidity, clarity, and the ability to move as a master, because only until self is defined can the master then be born. It can never be born out of undifferentiated self. Did you understand what I have just taught you? Did you understand about the core defining self and its power? You now understand that giving that power away depletes the core.

Notice that when I refer to the past, I always refer to your greatest obstacles. Seemingly in reference to that which is termed the past, it seems as if I think that the past was all terrible. No, it was all purposeful.

What I want you to understand is that all the beautiful things in your life — all of those things that you did and were done to you that are sweet — those could only have occurred in a moment of self-definition, so they are always with you because they are the core of what you are. That is the reason why, in religions, God is always pleading with his flock to be good and do good deeds and be men and women of moral and impeccable values, because there is a truth in that. The truth is that when you elect to be that way, you have not given any power away but have been empowered. The more that empowerment occurs, the more awesome the entity's reality. That is the way that it works. All of you are endeared with beautiful and sweet moments in your past. Those moments don't have to be thrown away because they are integral to defining the self.

If those defining moments are the lofty moments in your life, they can be seen as acts of the simplest things that you did from the moment of your cognitive memory of what was done to you and what you did to others all through your life. Those are empowering moments. That is the true self expressing. But for the most part, you live in a dynamic society to which blame and cowardliness in favor of an image is a way of life here. It is the dog-eat-dog, the hyena preying upon the young. It is success-motivated and feared by the aspects of failure. These then become the dynamic in a past that is grievous, a past in which power has been given away, in which victimization and blame and the pointing of fingers begin often at a very early age. You can see why it is important to address the past in terms of energy, in terms of giving it away and staying confined in a mode of consciousness and its neuronet of being the eternal sufferer and the eternal victim.

No master is this way, nor will you find sympathy from any master at your election to being this. Why? Because every master knows that every life's action is a personal choice and that personal choice is a free-willed choice. Any master who is a master understands and knows that, without sympathy or empathy. These are very clear distinctions in what you are learning here. The distinction is that the master has seated the self firmly in its divine room and from this point navigates that divinity towards a life that is based entirely upon the crucial, contemplative, meditative placement of energy. That is the master.

Judgment Day and the Life Review

Having said that now and reminding you that you are here by choice — that you chose this life as a life in which the spiritual would become revealed to you — is empowering you utterly. From this, I am going to back up and talk about the Plane of Bliss — heaven, as some would call it.

Over the years in your time we have discussed frequently the interim existence, that interim existence which you were prior to this incarnation. Although I have not lingered at great depth upon that existence or upon your past life, there is great and wonderful reason for that, for in my wisdom I understand that those who do not have spiritual maturity cling to these with the same values as they have clung to their victimization, their tyranny, and their self-pity. It is giving more fodder to the animal within man and woman than it is that which is termed manna for the spiritual self. The focus here has been on becoming God. That is what is important and will always be important, but now we are going to talk about the interim place and the place where all of you were before you were born.

I have stated boldly in the past that we do not create our parents. That is true. But remember that we are drawn to a genetic pool that is only equal to what we are before arriving. In that sense, subconsciously we only become what we are capable of becoming. We can never become what we are incapable of becoming. In other words, we cannot be anything greater than what we are. When we speak about the interim place, it refers to the third, fourth, and fifth levels. They are the planes of rest and restoration.

It becomes obvious that the physical body has died and all of its energy from the soul that gave it life is pulling away from it, and the body goes into a slow state of decay. Without modern technology and the art of embalming, the energy naturally would rapidly decay within a matter of a fortnight. Decay is the breaking down of coagulated matter and the release of the conscious pattern. We are talking about the self, the spiritual self, that which is not seen, that has already departed up through infrared into the great tunnel of light to be met by the lords of light at the very end. All of you went through the reading of your life. In elder times it was called Judgment Day. It is Judgment Day, except that it really isn't a judgment but to refresh your memory on what you did.

Now understand that you are a being that is transpersonal but still personal. You are a being that is transmuted out of a fleshy body. You have gotten out of the garment, and here, where there was such a delay in the Spirit working through the body to create reality — because you are living in a body that is mass to mass — now you are more in your own domain as a spiritual entity. You are actually vibrating in a kinder realm than this realm.

There you watch your life. How is that possible? Because the bands that you are — that supported, nourished, and gave life to you in the womb — take back with them, as mind, everything that you ever did, because doing is an action and action is energy, and the focus of that energy is the patterns of mind. You then begin to watch the patterns of mind as they come together in a whole lifetime's effort.

Now let's pause here for a moment and let me tell you this. Every moment — every moment — in the light of all eternity will be weighed against a feather one day. Every moment counts. Everything that you do and I did is seen, and it is seen both as the Observer and the participant, both as the doer and the done-to — everything. That is why it is called Judgment Day because most ignorant people think, or they are under the delusion, that their thoughts aren't things. Their thoughts are things, and they are under the delusion that what they do behind their closed doors no one knows but them. That is a delusion. Everything is known and everything will be shown. In this heightened state it is necessary not for any one being to look at you and condemn you; it will be enough that you see it for yourself. There is no harsher judge than the soul on Judgment Day.

When this occurs — and you are all at one point going to experience it because you have already experienced it — what is meaningful from it? What becomes meaningful is how burdened you are by unfinished business, how burdened you are by unfinished experiences. If I tell you that you are God, then this life is to evolve that Godhead as all. So how many experiences did you not own? Every time that you were cruel to someone, that you were cunning and undermining, every time that you bore false testimony against someone else, that you physically hurt someone, that your tongue lashed out in revenge and blame, that you meted out your fury of unrequited love to the destruction of those around you and yourselves, everything becomes you in that moment of viewing. You are everything.

You suffer the attack of your villainy and you feel what it feels like. You become the child that you have beaten and you feel its helpless pain. You become that which is termed the abuser and the full onslaught of tempted, intoxicating fury upon that which is innocent and cannot strike back. You feel what it is to be slandered upon and your good and gracious name abused and dishonored. You will feel that because you are God.

We are not separate in this hour. We are whole in this hour. We are driven to understanding, more than any other time, that it is in this passing we realize that we are the whole web of life. We feel the abandonment of that which we have abandoned. We feel the untruth that we are upon someone else. We feel the blame placed upon us unduly by ourselves. We feel that which is termed the heartbreak of unrequited love, and we are the one who bore the chains of that blame. We are honored and dishonored. We are amused and bemused. We see how we prostituted our values. We become the body in its agony and in its abuse. We become the abuser and the abused, and this is judgment and we feel it full-width. We revel in the dream and in the inspiration that we had at five, and we despair in the losing of that dream at twenty-three. We become the dream and then we fade as the dream. We become the inspiration that we marveled at and then we become the boredom of inaction. We see the instigation of new ideas, concepts that we came up with — we are then the idea itself, the thought-form — and we see it as an unnurtured, unloved egg that never hatches. We see the idea that never came into fruition and the pain of its noninclusiveness into our environment. We see it all because we are all God.

The subjective element in all of this is very important. The core of self is subjective because it is everything, so the self becomes more enriched and more defined in this view. We see how many times we needed to beg someone's pardon and we see all the times we didn't ask it of ourselves. We see all the times that we could have loved, but in our selfish, renegade selves meted none out, and we see the vacuous place where love lives not and we are driven in emptiness and despair. We see it all.

In this exposé we find wholeness even in the suffering, that rarefied moment. And how do I describe suffering without a body? Emotion, though it is generated by electrical stimuli from the brain, from neuronets, that then have a domino effect in the body through the release of hormones, becomes a living thing. It is an energy field, and it is with that energy field that we stand in the light review and we are then immersed within all of this energy. We cannot undo it. It is done. The die has been cast.

Now this is not a bad thing but is necessary for the ignorant — and you all are — because what we do with such a vision is that we then become encumbered. We become encumbered by the difficulties in which we see ourselves. An encumbrance is a wonderful term because what it really says is that we did all of these things to ourselves. It is through this revelation that we must unencumber and give to the self love, which God is. Remember, God is giving.

Mapping Our New Life on the Plane of Bliss

We walk away from this in deep ponderance. We are given any sort of image with which we wish to ponder this. Some ponder on high mountain ranges on Bliss. Some ponder behind great and noble trees, by beautiful lakes surrounded by dappled woods, in great libraries, or floating in the midst of nothing because they can't tolerate anything to be around them. But ponderance, the art of contemplation, always follows this, and what becomes inescapable is that we have done this to ourselves because we are all the self.

Now here is the stickler. These acts in this life grew out of a very slow time and the whole focal point was the human body, so no matter what you do on the Plane of Bliss, you can never reconcile there what you did on the plane of flesh. We cannot manifest on the Plane of Bliss the experiences that will bring about physical emotion because we are without them.

We contemplate and then imagine, like I did by the fire in dreaming this journey. We imagine, and as soon as we imagine, all of the forms and the scenes appear, and they appear instantly. As we contemplate, we watch ourselves and how we deal with what we dealt out. We imagine, and because we are on the Plane of Bliss where there is no mass to mass, we are more akin to that time, which is no-time as it is referred to here. The moment that we imagine something there, it appears exactly as we imagine it, so our surroundings are always changing.

In contemplation this is ideal, because when we contemplate we can visually see the exact scene and how we would like it to happen. Try as we may, however, to get relief from that, we cannot get relief from it. What it does provide us with is our divinity. Our gift to image has allowed us to reconstruct the past, to reconstruct the past and move from that point forward. However, this mapping, though thoroughly researched, could take thousands of years on Bliss. Contemplation on Bliss is much different than contemplation here. We may linger there and plot and plan, and we may seek it out in these planes. The moment the idea occurs to us that there are these great beings with wisdom, they appear and teach us. They help with our model of imagination. They do not change the model in the time of contemplation. The thoughts are given to you and you incorporate the wisdom into the picture. That is how it works, because it is not their picture; it is your picture.

Knowledge: If knowledge to you means a reservoir of information flowing through a computer, a computer will appear which will have dendrites connected to you and the knowledge will flow through the computer. But ultimately in the knowledge flowing back to you, you must be the program that incorporates it. You may envision knowledge in great halls of learning, in the great halls of academia. You may envision this knowledge in a set of rare books so immediately a great library will appear and you will not be able to see the end of it, and yet all of the great texts appear on old and ancient shelves. In your mind, old may mean that they are faded and covered in dust and so they will be. You look for the dustiest, faded, cobweb-covered manual you can find, because in your mind that is the one that will have all knowledge, and you will find it. You will have a table where you can sit down. You can have an electric lamp, a candle, an oil lamp, a florescent lamp, and you sit down and read. You read every page, a page that looks like soft light, and letters that are multidimensional and they jump off the page into you and you think you are reading. It is all the same knowledge.

What you walk away from, in spending a hundred years in this library, is information on how to modulate the room of contemplation, the room of how you are going to make it different, to elongate this burden that you have of being unfinished, the error as you see it that you have done to another. How you would be able to justify that and how you would be able to write it, you will figure it all out. Now it is not by accident that this is starting to act exactly like a quantum field of potential because it is. The Plane of Bliss is at the quantum level. When an entity that is spiritual — without the body — is rarefied mind, the moment occurs immediately. What the entity is doing is selecting paths of intentional destiny, creating them in a linear fashion with or without the help and endeavoring to find a resolve, because no one wants to live being all things punished and punishable. That realm is called hell, but one lives in it as unresolved, burdened, unfinished business.

Keep in mind there is no one on this plane that will ever say you are right and wrong. You are the ones that do that. There is no right and wrong. It becomes immensely clear to us that we are of the angelic realm, that we really are foreign travelers in an alien world, and that we really are empowered to re-create that world according to our imagination, our greatest resource. No one there is to say this is right and wrong. I tell you the more God you are in that moment of light review, you will feel the blow of everything measured out by you in incarnation, because how could God be anything else but everything?

In the hall of contemplation — this is very important — there are beings that are still there that have been mapping a potential lifetime very carefully. They have been there for hundreds of thousands of years. They are mapping it. They are like the watcher-at-the-gate story I told you about, one who watches everyone coming in.[5] There are entities that post themselves at heaven's great gate and watch everyone coming

5 The source of this story is in Ramtha, *Selected Stories III: Shambhala — Leaving No Footprints*. Specialty Audiotape 033 edition (Yelm: Ramtha Dialogues, 1989).

in with all their stuff, and they learn. But what is important is that it is not meaningful learning until it is applied on the level in which the wisdom was generated.

I am telling you about a plane, in ordinary tongue, that is much more illustrious, much more dynamic, much more fantastic, and much more beautiful than this common speech can allow. I am endeavoring to bring it home to you, a very valuable lesson which you are learning about the remarkable self and understanding why you chose to be here.

An encumbered entity who has a lot of unfinished business here, unless they have a physical body working in this time they cannot finish it. They can dream it on those other levels but those dreams will never be able to be experienced until they are born in the time to which they were meant. An encumbered entity there has drawn out the linear path and received as much help as they know to ask, and when they are ready to return, they are drawn into genetic pools that are equal to what they left behind.

In this Plane of Bliss — in heaven, as some would call it, the greater planes I call them — there is no regret at being there. I want you to know that never was a place more lively and more beautiful than this because it is the unimaginable imagined. Never was there such a state of being that utterly was free of the encumbrances of slow time and slow matter. Never was there a place where physical beauty wasn't the most important thing, because there you could take on any appearance that you wanted so it isn't important, but here it is important. There it is not important because it is changeable. Everyone is free from that, so you are floating closer to God. You are in a state shadowed by the golden realm. You are in a state where it can be the eternal day or the eternal night. There are multitudes there, and it seems as if there is room for everyone, and there is. It is a deserving place to be. It is the place of rest before the next battle.

It is not unlike some of you, who are prone to suffering anyway, to see it as a place where you linger in the contemplative forests and suffer. No, but that is important as the subjective aspect of God to be able to feel what you did, but you are always objective. And from that, there is no grief about leaving your family. There is no grief about leaving your husbandmen, your wives, your friends, your neighbors. You don't have that sort of emotion because you are free of all of that.

There is a knowingness that permeates these realms, that what is happening on the Earth plane is a great big drama and you played a part. What is important is that you never finished your lines and that coming out of that thick dream, you know your children were not left behind. They will always be. Coming out of that, you didn't leave behind your love. Your love is with you, always will be, because when we become the subjective God, we interface with all life, so how could we be separate from it? It is such a state that it is difficult to understand, but you have all been there. You have all been there; otherwise you couldn't be here now.

Now stop grieving and suffering for a moment and understand that this encumbered state is what generates us to our greater power. We want to design a life and lay it out and imagine it and change the patterns, the players. Anyone that wants to volunteer can move into it. We want to do that before we return and pick up where we left off. Now that is very important as well.

I want to back up and talk about the players involved in the upcoming drama. What has always been considered is that people who meet and have a kinship for one another met in a past life. That is not so. Try this one on: How about that you never met before and met on the Plane of Bliss because you had both come through the same encumbrance, you both arrived at the same forest to contemplate the same thing? Some of these places are very crowded — very crowded — and we always gravitate to what we are. The players that will play an integral part in the upcoming life don't have to be anyone that we were before, and to always delude yourselves into thinking that shows the sign of your ignorance about the spiritual life, because this place isn't everything and these lifetimes aren't everything. We will have beings that will meet in the same place of contemplation that may be extraordinarily advanced entities whose past incarnations were geniuses or great leaders, and they have a flaw, which flaw brought them in contact with you. They may be coming instead from another terrestrial planet in which they can work out that flaw on this one. We meet through association of encumbrances.

How difficult is this to understand that when you sit by someone and you engage them in a conversation, you are bonding with them and pretty soon you are moving through the labyrinth of their mind, understanding what they are saying to you. You are into them and they in turn are moving through the labyrinth of your mind. That is what we call conversation. If you understand that, then you can begin to grasp the concept that association of encumbrances brings like to like, and when shared upon in that rarefied place — it is not about talking, you don't talk — your thoughts are proclaimed and so each of you engages in each other's thoughts. It is at those times that engaging in each other's thoughts we find a marvelous and wonderful thing happens called mercy. In this wonderful kingdom — this life that we have laid out for ourselves — we have found someone who has the same encumbrance, but the encumbrance may be that that entity had done unto them what we did to others. Although we are both done-to-and-did in this place of contemplation, our minds come together and formulate a relationship, and those relationships then form a later meeting on this plane.

It is not about who you knew two thousand years ago or four thousand years ago. The most meaningful ones are the ones that you meet on Bliss because they have arrived at the same place. These people will come in and out of your life often to fulfill the very drama that you came back here to play out. And which role are they playing now? It is ultimately selected at that moment. When they viewed their life and they did an unthinkable to someone else, they can restrategize so that the unthinkable then is done to them, and the player that will be involved is one who was the victim in the earlier existence. They are learning balance, and yet they only may appear and then disappear out of your life, but that is what they are here to do. There is no such thing as chance. Everything is created from consciousness, and consciousness does not simply hold itself and its sole purpose on this plane; it is all planes. The closer we are to Point Zero, the more pure we are as conscious beings. In this great and wonderful realm — that the moment you think it, it is — is our true nature. That is our true nature. That is what we are used to. What we are not used to is being bogged down and burdened by slow time and the mechanics of the physical body, because there we are liberated from it and all that it represents.

When we set out in our memorable engagement with other beings there — when we set this pattern out and we have decided upon this potential line — then we are ready to return. Those that we have blended with before, we will meet again. We won't remember them but we will meet them, and the soul will know because the Spirit recalls the conversation. The soul recalls the journey. It is just the corporal mind — the corporal brain of the physical entity — which is yet to be born that will not remember this incident.

The Value of Experiencing a New Incarnation

When we are ready, we come back because we can go no further unless we come back here and take care of this unfinished business, until we understand completely that God is one. When we are one — when we decide to be one — is when we have selected the spiritual journey, a life filled with that. Now understand also that there are entities on these planes that although they too are burdened down by encumbrances, their greatest encumbrance is the lack of success because they never got to be that, so they are naturally going to formulate lines of potential to which they are born. They are born in the backwater and they have to move through this life and become a success from out of shambles. That is the way their drama will be played out. It is very important for them, and someone must be the fall guy in the play. Do you know why they must be the fall guy? Because those are the entities that stepped on other people to attain success in their previous lifetime and so the meaningful minds come together for this wonderful display.

There are people whose encumbrances are the lack of success, for example, and they are going to lay down that potential of a whole life in a large sandbox to which they play the game for that one fleeting moment of glory, and that is all the life would have been worth — that fleeting moment. Then the life becomes degenerated because it will reflect only on that one moment and it will become its past.

Now that you understand encumbrances a little bit better, you begin to see that those entities we have met in this lifetime were not met by accident, that each person we met along the way was actually part of a line potential that we created on Bliss. What is interesting about the mapping on Bliss is that it very rarely ever acts out on Earth like it did on Bliss. We have a tendency to paint things very cheery on Bliss. We forgot what it felt like to have a blister on our hands from gripping too tight. We forgot what it was like holding too tight. We don't know that. That is why in the material realm when all of this falls into place, it is a remarkable adventure because its maturation is much different than how we planned it before, and then we have the element of the bare mystery of enchanted forgetfulness that also plays into it and is supposed to play into it. Therefore all lives that come together in this life aren't necessarily recognized from before, and you shouldn't try to do that because in trying to do that, sometimes you may muddy the picture of the potential that you are endeavoring to find here. We are endeavoring to find self. We are endeavoring to do it with clarity and purity, without any pollution whatsoever, to find the rawest of our beautiful nature. The more that we can demystify it, the more real it will become.

In order to reconcile every situation, when we try to frame it in cosmic text we oftentimes muddy the picture. Relationships don't have to be cosmic; that is a joke. They only need to be relationships. We are going to come closer to the plan from that raw and dynamic center than if we tried to take it out of context and make it into something it never was, because then we find the encumbrances of creating phantoms that only begin to bother us. In reality, oftentimes in every life that fulfills the contemplation room that we create — however long, however complicated, however short — our true and wonderful friends are really the emergence from the future, never the past, because on the Plane of Bliss is where the future is born.

Most individuals start out with good intentions, and their plan never comes into real fruition because they get stuck.

Now this is an important message about the past. When you get stuck in the past you deny yourselves your future potential, and that is what is so grievous about your acts of holding onto your victimization, your suffering, your anguish, your parents did this or did that. Why sacrifice what was created on Bliss for holding onto that which is temporal in the flesh?

When we give our power away to enslaving factors of yesterday, we diffuse the self for and from which we created the potential on Bliss. When we no longer have self because we have disempowered it through grief, suffering, misery, anxiety, and all of that, we stop the flow of our true destiny and all we get is the garbage that we cling to for the sake of self-identity. And why not do that when it has served you well so far? It has enslaved lovers. It has made people feel sorry for you. You have used it to get your way. You have used it against other people. You have used it upon yourselves. It has served you. Why would you want to get rid of it? Because unless you do, you don't get the great future that you have created for yourselves and all the marvelous beings that joined you in its creation and you with them — who will touch your lives in unimaginable ways, who will move your soul in waves of fire you have never known, who will inspire you towards your ingenious self — of which no one hereto of your past has been able to do.

You designed a destiny to unencumber yourself, and in that the great minds participated in the making. When we release ourselves to that, we get out of the way and let it come. Our clinging nature to yesterday only is going to take us back through this process and we are going to still be encumbered by what we have not met and, for a very materialistic term, we are going to be the lesser for the greatness we denied ourselves made in heaven.

In other words, so many lifetimes are just repetitious — repeating the same cyclical movements that are born in the soul, the same experiences that the cowardliness of the human element backs away from — and do not allow the pristine movement of the soul to finish, take its power back, and then make room for a marvelous destiny.

Now why do we do this? That "why" is a very broad understanding that takes lifetimes to comprehend, but I taught it to you in your first C&E®. You are explorers from Point Zero. You are making known the unknown. What is important is to imagine the dream and to bring it into fruition, give birth to it in an impossible, arduous, and difficult realm. The dream must exist on all seven levels in order to be fully realized by the dreamer. When we are down here casting dreams in thick time, we are down here casting dreams in a thick time that we are not used to. We are creatures of an eternal imagination because that is how we are. We are consciousness and energy. We are builders of archetypes of thought, and from that then energy behaves to form those thoughts, to become their movement, if you will.

We are not creatures of the flesh. We never have been. When we allow our flesh to give us away — to give us away — and to fracture our divinity into personalities that hold old fires, old flames, old bitterness, unresolved and unyielding, we are fractured. We are — listen to me carefully — the self called God, and when we allow our bodies to fracture us, our power then is split as brother against brother. We are at war to our very nature. We are no longer whole and pristine. We are here to make known the unimaginable, not to rehash what is already known and to warp its sense of maturity into a state that degrades even us.

On this Plane of Bliss we get to carry with us our most recent likeness. Oftentimes it is very helpful because like the great scar on my front and my back helped to remind me always of my own inflicted treachery, we get to keep our bodies in their most recent form to remind us of what we must unencumber, or we can simply choose to be nebulous in form. However we want to present ourselves, we may present ourselves in that fashion. But while we are on the Plane of Bliss, we are in a state of bliss. We are in a state of communion with the highest levels of life, and we are ever so close to the fountainhead of it all — the eternal Point Zero, as it has come to be known — the whole unifying with the Void itself. On Bliss we are enjoying each other's company. We are enjoying the bliss, the harmony, the magic of a mind. We are that mind. We are that most divine revelation of imagination as it stands before us, as it twists and turns and changes at our every thought. That is what we really are and always have been.

Why then would you come down here just to live a couple of years so that we could work out something? Is it really worth it? Of course it is worth it. When you know you are eternal, playing the part even for a year is worth it. What isn't worth it? Our point here is that we are the little Gods that tried but got caught. We got caught — and in what I have been endeavoring to teach you about ever since you have been with me — we got caught in a garment, that its whole nature is so utterly backward from our very own, who has to exist in this slow-moving, slow-time, compelling existence that has alienated us from what our whole nature actually is.

We have to finish our business, not so that we can go home. We have to finish our encumbrances so that we can be free of this entanglement of our cowardly nature of human flesh, that we can finish up what the nature of the human has not been able to do.

CHAPTER 5
MAKING THE CHOICE THAT ENDURES
INTO ETERNITY

"I am here to tell you what you are — and you
get to make choices from that — and to give you
excellent knowledge that you can start to integrate,
to give you hope, and to keep reminding you I am
talking to Gods out here. I am talking to immortals
that are so powerful they can believe themselves into
eternal death. That is how powerful you are.
I am talking to Gods."
— *Ramtha*

The Animal Nature of Humanity

I want to tell you something. When it is said that the human is an animal, that is correct. The human is an animal because of its animal nature: the nature of strong survival, strong reproduction, and being highly territorial. Some are solitary predators, are cunning, and strike from behind. They are not brave. The weak gather together in greater numbers to protect their boundaries, hoping that someone else will fall but not them. This is the animal nature.

How close are you to that nature? I can tell you how close you are. The spiritual nature isn't even working when you launch an attack upon the innocent, when you flail your debtors with a cat-o'-nine-tails because they owe you, when you hate because you give. You are territorial because you want to protect your boundaries, and you would jump at the chance to copulate. That is the animal. The body does that very well because that is the nature of the kingdom from which it is derived. Brave men and women who are acting in a role of greatness never attack from behind. Only a coward and a predator, who are both the same, do that. If that is the way that this is — and who can deny it — how far are you really from it other than having good table manners, wearing garments, and that you defecate in toilets and not on the plains? You are not that far removed from your animal nature. The first three seals are the animal nature. When that human has its way, it will always act like an animal because it is a coward. I tell you it is the spiritual self — what I am telling you that you really are — that is the only viable aspect of this incarnation that can truly address encumbrances and is equipped to handle them. The human is not. You know, you are a coward who lived in a tarnished past of suffering. That is your cowardliness. You are an animal. If you have not been relieved from it or been strong enough to relieve yourselves of it, then you have yet to be a spiritual person because the Spirit is what is best equipped to do this because it is after it. The Spirit is after the encumbrances because, first, it has to take its power back to regain its wholeness of self. When it does, it is the one that says, "No more. This is finished. I created it. I am responsible for it. I forgive you. You are free." That is a spiritual person. But what does the animal say? "You owe me. And now that you are vulnerable, I am going to get you." That is the animal.

Being an altered ego is not going to help you. Just because you are born down here, your genetics are not in your favor because they came from genetics that were trying to do the same thing. And, remember, you are only drawing the physical body that was closest to what you were. This is a continuing story. We come back here not because anybody sent us back here; we sent ourselves. We are back here not to change the world but to change ourselves. We are back here to be realized, not to be forgotten again. We have come back here to finish up this business.

Now I want to ask you in light of what I have taught you about the Plane of Bliss, it becomes monumental that these little heart tremors of the personality carry more weight than you could possibly know, does it not? It is not the success we accomplish on this plane that is remembered in the halls of Bliss. It is not about how much money you make or how much you don't make. It is not about how famous you were or how infamous you were. It is not about what you look like. It is not about any of that that is so important here. What is important is what we did do. It is important enough to bring Gods to human knees because our agenda is different than the human animal. Our agenda is to be unencumbered and then bring in the unimaginable. That is what this is about. Have people before you done that? Indeed there have been. There have been people who have cleaned up their experiences, finalized them, and were free of them. Who were they? The brilliant people that are now scattered and peppered throughout history that were geniuses because they brought the unimaginable through. They had the power to do it because self was put back on the throne. It was gathered back together, pieced together, and put on the throne.

Very few of these individuals that are heroic in your history got there by Bliss. Most of them paid dearly for their genius. In other words, they suffered, endured, proclaimed, and accomplished. They took the tiger on, and that turbulent life led to the one thing they wanted to accomplish here, the unimaginable, that they already knew before they were incarnated here. They got above the human drama and became Gods once again, and if only for a moment their star shined, that is all it took. It was over with then. It is finished, which brings me back to my introduction to you.

You made the choice to be here and to choose spiritual learning in this life. I set the foundation and you came. There is one great union that all of us in this school, save for a few, have in common. We shared collectively a lifetime together, a very tumultuous, arduous, awe-inspiring, great life and you witnessed marvelous things: the ending of an old Earth and the beginning of a new one. You witnessed the dying of the Gods and the birth of humankind, and you marched the long march. That is what we share in common and for that, love borne throughout the pages of this march resides to this moment. That allowed this moment to have a place in the Void in the mind of God, that when you were ready to choose to know more, there was a place to come. It was inevitable.

Why, on the Plane of Bliss, in heaven, would you choose what you already are on the Plane of Bliss to realize down on this plane if you already know it up there? Good question? Yes, it is, because what is realized up there in order to be fully known must be realized into the bowels of God, and it has to be made known here because this is the cauldron, the alchemist's crucible. The shining star dancing on midnight-blue liquid suddenly recoagulates and comes down to that little ball of nickel in the bottom of the bowl again. So here we are. You have to do it here.

On the Plane of Bliss most all of you came through your labyrinth and your encumbrances. You still have encumbrances but all of you had a place of love in you, a place through which to vacillate. You had something startling happen to you. You saw me leave the plane without dying. You never forgot that. Where did I go and how did I escape the decay and the rottenness of the body? How was I able to do that? You got to see that. That is why the legend of Christ and the resurrection are so strong in Christian minds today. It is poignant because it is a longing. It is an unimaginable imaginable that has set its seed in the minds of many people. You will find this in all religious doctrine.

With me and my people, before all of that gibberish, I left and you saw it and that was it, in my true style. Make a point and get on, which makes you ask, "Where did he go? He is not on the Plane of Bliss. Where is he?" Well, I am on the Plane of Bliss. When you came back, before you got back, you remembered me and where I went. Love is unforgettable. It is so sweet. It is unforgettable because it lacks nothing, so in your labyrinth you asked the ultimate question, "What is the unimaginable for me?"

Now there is another group across the river asking the same question. That is the group that invented computers. That group is just now discovering that if they can create an idea on the superplane of existence and move it right along into the timeline — that if they get it in this body they are about to be born into and it actually works — whether you know it or not those technological geniuses are starting to wake up to what you are already getting to know. In other words, they are behind you. They look like they are in front of you but they are actually behind you because they are just learning to create. They are just learning what you already know.

This group then says what do I need to know? With what do I need to unencumber myself? Well, you are asking a heap but, after all, all you are asking for is unfinished business. When it is done, what do you want? I want to go where no human has gone before. I want to know. I want to go where the Gods dwell. I want to know what it is to be a master, and when you imagined what a master was, you thought of me. When you thought of the dale of the Gods, you thought of me and created in your mind where you thought I went. This fascinating journey — this fascinating puzzle, this exercise, this toy labyrinth that you built in your potential imagination — got you strung out on being spiritual because, you see, you don't get it unless you ask for it. Somewhere along the way there must be an ideal which comes into human consciousness that trips it. All through your history you have had wonderful beings that have come in and circumvented the system, that have been so bold, so arrogant, so pure as to stand ten feet above the mediocre human. What made them so different was because they were filled with the power of the Holy Spirit instead of the power of the animal. That is what made them different. Why did they come back? They came back to reremind you, "Never forget me. I am going to make such an impression on you that you are never going to forget me because one day you are going to want to know what I am."

Redefining the Self by Choosing Our Spiritual Nature

I am an ideal. It has been necessary to sprinkle ideals historically for all civilizations to keep them from collapsing — some astonishing thing that happened at noon, an appearance or reappearance of phenomena — something to snap us from this heavy melatonin dream of the carnal life, that wakes us up and then we click on in the brain. When we click on, we click on as spiritual beings and click off as human beings. I was your catalyst.

In the light of all eternity, why would you want to spend this lifetime developing your spiritual self? First you have to overcome your encumbrances, own the past, because it says to you — those of you who make it — that you really have come to understand that you have already done everything in human consciousness. My God, who haven't you been, what haven't you had? Who haven't you hated and how many haven't you loved? How many times do you have to die? How many times do you have to get sick? How many times do you need to be successful to realize you never were a failure? How many times does it take? Only an entity coming back here would know that the only reason you come back here is because you must finish your business, but your unimaginable dream is to be the superbeing. What greater dream is there than God? There is none.

You included this in your potential line and remembered me from an incident I had with you. That is what brought this into being and you chose it. You want to understand what has not been you and you want to find deliverance from your burden and wholeness. That wholeness speaks to a wholeness of the self, that once it is completely contained it will be ready for the emergence of the future that was created on the Plane of Bliss.

Everyone has character flaws; everyone does. But to what scale of perfection do we find flaws? No one here is perfect. There is no such thing as the perfect human. No matter how hard you try, you will never get there because in order to be that, you are going to have to be as base as any animal and you are already too far-gone the other way.

You came here through a line that you created on the Plane of Bliss to learn not what was already here but what could be here. You came to have something bring up and remind you of the experiences that you need to complete. Those can be completed as simply as you wish or as arduously as you wish. You can then from that be utterly and totally free to incorporate what you have already created, an unimaginable beauty. I promise you, no one ever goes backwards when they are free of their encumbrances. They are truly liberated. They are liberated from their animal, from their suffering. They become whole. They find the self, that which they really are.

I told you three times in this teaching that our natural way of creating is instantaneously. You begin to understand why a God would become so fractured in a human, because what we get immediately has to be processed into coagulation for the human. The human is always protecting boundaries, always checking out victims, looking for survival, and always needing the copulation. These are impatient qualities. Nature is the survival of the fittest. And when it comes to the animal, the animal must be as the fittest in all of these categories. When we truly become human beings, we really fracture the holy in ourselves because the impatient human cannot hold onto an unimaginable imaginable if that dream does not directly relate to its security, sovereignty, longevity, its basis of copulation, and its superiority among unequals. The human will never hold a dream that does not facilitate its animal nature. That is the reason why the human is impatient and always riddled with doubt when it comes to imagination. And here we are, the very Gods that made this creature. We revel in the imagination as true reality but cannot enjoy it to the root of God on this plane because the body that we inhabit cannot hold onto it and rejects it, thereby denying us access to that experience. The body is not a dreamer. It can create thoughts. It is the computer. It can hold them holographically, but it finds it tiring to hold onto them. The God is the moment, it is the dreamer, and it needs to be strong enough in the body to be able to bring the dream forth instead of emasculating it.

This is a battle because what always happens is that the body wins and the Spirit loses, so there you go into a fall, into another meaningless life. The only thing you are going to do when you die is go back and see the same program over and have to go and address it in the same contemplation. You will be happy and relieved, but there is a greater calling for you even there.

You are unfinished here. The spiritual journey and the walk of the master start when very painful issues must be addressed: the nature of the human and the nature of the Spirit, its destiny, how it is perceived as both human and spiritual. What is important to the human will not be important to the Spirit. What the human finds subjective and personal, the Spirit will find objective and impersonal. You also have bodies that can't hold dreams and give up because they are prancing their territory. They have to keep moving to keep their boundaries safe, and you have a God who is endeavoring to get the experience.

When you choose to have a life where you dedicate it to your spiritual revelation, you are asking for a life in which you must ride those horses of the sensual self with a tight rein. In that life the Spirit must be developed. The painful process of taking back one's power often means tripping up the body, its family roots. It means pulling out from under it its own rug of blame and jealousy, the dynamics of family situations, sexuality, prejudice, and saying in an unequal yet singular tone, "I created this. It never was your fault. I made you think it was your fault because that is the coward in me. I blamed you for feeling less about myself when it had nothing to do with you. I inflicted the lack of self-love upon me and indeed it is I who have rejected myself and cloistered myself. I am the one who left you; you never left me. I am the one who has wallowed in self-pity and lingered in my past. You never were in my present because I was never there. I was gone. I was in yesterday. It is not your fault. It is just a habit I have." It takes great spiritual depth to be an honorable man and an honorable woman. It hurts deeply, but I would rather feel the coming back of the wind of begotten energy moving through the emotional body and getting purified to make us whole rather than never be whole at all.

I talked to you about intense clarity, pure and unobstructed, and that every thought is meted out decisively. It is never simply taken for randomness but it is contemplated so much until the extraordinary and lofty way to think becomes the common way to think. That is hard to do, especially when your body tells you that you are missing a lot. It is hard to stay in the dark night of the soul without stimulus to get you out of it. But why would you want to get out of it? It is pulling that energy back from those painful places that must pass through the emotional body. That is where the true suffering is but that is also where purification happens. To dull it, to get rid of it, would deny yourself purification and thus wisdom.

What is wrong with processing energy? Don't you think you are strong enough to do it? True, the human being is an impatient critter. It is a nasty one too when it is cornered. But are you such a coward that you can't deal with the issues that you have created? After all, they will never be greater than you because they came from you. Or is it that you can deal it out but you can't take it when it comes back? Is that what a drug really is, to numb the sensation of the return of what you meted out? I would think about that if I were you.

The Spiritual Walk of the Master

O my beloved God,
unto me this day
move as my Holy Spirit
to draw me up
into your realm
and hold me there.
O my beloved God,
let my Spirit
flow from my being
unencumbered.
I accept this knowledge
in freedom.
I desire its revelation
unto me.
O my beloved God,
I am thankful
for my life.
O my beloved God,
I am thankful
for my body.

My beloved God,
fill me with your love
eternally,
and God bless my life.
So be it.
To life.

Let's do a little review of this wonderful teaching about self and heaven. We will start off in the right frame of consciousness. We want to evolve this so that we can gain deeper knowledge. Let's start with the knowledge that we had and set our minds on a righteous path to understanding.

The first teaching I gave you was that you chose to be here, to come and learn a spiritual understanding. No one made you come. You are here because this is what you want to learn. Self-choice is the beginning of self-empowerment or the redefinition of self. The second thing that you learned was defining self. You are still a little hazy about self, and it is only a term. These words that I use are only words. What is important now is reminding you what I taught about learning to hear and why it was important that a master teaches you.[6] A master can teach you, and if you are hearing, what is it causing to occur in your brain? Pictures, holograms. That is the way to hear. These words stimulate the brain to create pictures, and as you also learned, true self is imagination, the act of imaging. That is our destiny. That is what we are supposed to do. If you then listen today, you will be helped to redefine perhaps old definitions because as I talk, and if you can stay with me, your brain is going to produce the pictures that my words, properly placed, are going to occur in your brain, and if they do, then you are now thinking in spiritual terms.

6 See Ramtha, *Fireside Series, Vol. 2, No. 1, Crossing the River* (Yelm: JZK Publishing, 2002).

To learn the definition of self, we must go all the way back to Point Zero, to what I taught when you first came to see me: You are God, and then of course we have to redefine what God is and remove from it the shackles of limitation and dogma. We use that which is termed physics to be able to explain the metamorphosis of involution as well as evolution, reality. Self is a pure, creative state of consciousness and its handmaiden energy, inextricably combined. Consciousness and energy is what we really, really are, and the self creating is none other than the Godhead itself. That is what we are.

If we understand then that we are not really the faces that we wear and we are not really the garment that we wear — and, moreover, we really aren't the territories that we define — then we start to see self in its most pure origin. We understand that self is not the subjective body in which we exist but that it is the objective mind of one and all reality. With this brain that has the ability to contemplate the infinite, even on its finite terms, you begin to see that our spiritual self has been a rolling culmination of the very experiences that it created. Now listen to what I said, that the Spirit is the rolling culmination of the very experiences that it has created in its eons of manifestation. What that essentially means is that the self is a broad mind — a mind, really — a mind that is made up of all of its consciousness and energy that it created. To move through a creation and not finish it would be a fracturing of that self and, remember, that is what we are. We as consciousness and energy, the Godhead itself, have only one real destiny — real destiny — and that is to make known the unknown. The more that we do so to imagine the unimaginable, the greater our unity as God, as oneness, becomes. That is what we are supposed to do. We are an ocean seeping into the shores of the Void, and we should be expanding that which we are. That is what the self is.

If we are an enigma, a mystifying, etherical quality called consciousness and energy, then the soul is what captures and holds forever the final experience, the final movement of that experience. It is the soul and the holding of that experience in its finality that allow consciousness to be so broad. Without the soul helping to define mind, we would only be creating, moving through the creation, and as soon as we have moved through it, we would be back where we were originally because we have created no margin of static reality from which to build other concepts. We have then the soul of memorable experience within the conscious-energy self. It is the quality that allows our mind to grow and to expand. It gives us our finished business which we use as springboards to create the next unimaginable. Now that is self, and it is awesome and powerful.

When we know that about what we are, we can see clearly why a life coming out of the wilderness and the murk and mire, a life that is born here in which the pursuit, destiny, and goal of that life is to find out what we are, is the loftiest life we will ever live. When we begin to imagine ourselves not in the eyes of humanity but begin to define ourselves in much broader terms, unimaginable terms, we start to locate what we are. That is the discovery of who we are. It is time to take a look at what is true and real about ourselves. That is what we call the spiritual life. That is the spiritual life.

In defining self, you also learned that self is in the body of an incarnation like yours and that self, when it was on the Plane of Bliss last time and every time from every incarnation, arrives there at heaven. The great agenda there — the great Judgment Day, the hour of judgment — is to see for yourselves, both subjective and objective, those aspects of how you placed energy and how ultimately you affected the central core of your being. You like to call it past-life review in its flowery, cosmic term.

What is important about that is in this hour of judgment, there is no one there in heaven, on Bliss, that is the judge. What we are is ourselves, and we have found that what covers up self is unfinished business.

You learned about the term called encumbrances, to be encumbered. When you view your past life and what you are going to do in this one, you are going to see everything. There is nothing that was ever forgotten in energy because every act was preceded by a thought, and that is what is real. The thought is real because it is what self is. It is consciousness and energy, and nothing is wasted. In reviewing your life, you review what is real. You see everything that you did, what you thought you were doing behind closed doors or behind the placid face of indifference or smiling emptiness. You begin to see it not only as you who did it and were thinking it, but consciousness and energy from this point of view, as self, is both. You not only get to see subjectively what you were thinking but also get to feel it subjectively as energy and where it was headed because we are, as you have learned, one. God is one mind. What we do, we do to ourselves regardless of the players. The players are ourselves, because that is how large self is.

You learned that what you do to someone else, you have done to yourself. In victimizing and being unmerciful, uncaring, entrapping, enslaving, being decadent, uncharitable, and unforgiving, you have done that to yourself. In the light review you get to feel what that feels like. Everything is energy and therefore you are the creators of that energy. Then it is your expulsion of that energy that comes home to you. That is Judgment Day. And why is it a painful moment? Because you really get to see every facet of yourself and the dynamics of that facet. You become the injured that you have injured, the enslaved that you enslaved. You are the victim of your abuse and feel it on every corner. The reason why that is important is because in order to do any of these acts in a lifetime, you must have a divine quality that you can utilize with which to do it. In other words, every act is preceded by a thought and the thought is coming from the divine Source inside of us; hence the act is us.

Remember that your encumbrances are giving your power away, fracturing your God, and being unwhole. Defining self in the spiritual life is about being in pursuit of the knowledge that allows you to address your encumbrances. It allows you in the spiritual life to find out who you are, and it is important that you do so. You never walk as angels in the beginning of this spiritual journey. You come humbly with your dead mules at the door — your hauntings, phantoms, sufferings, your anxieties — and the devil that you bring with you is your altered ego.

You learn that the spiritual life is about taking your power back. Of everything I have taught you, the essential message is regaining coherently the power that you have fractured away because when you do, you dismantle the temple within; you dismantle the godhood within. Every block, every golden stone that makes up the temple of the self, has been given to all of these particular areas that constitute an inordinate amount of suffering. You are separated from your God because your God is fractured around you. That is an encumbrance. In order to do the unimaginable, you have to rebuild this temple. You have to redefine yourself, and that is not easy. Where have you given your power away and what does that mean? It doesn't mean giving it to somebody to control your life, although that is an aspect of it. It doesn't really mean that. It is a finer, more mystical meaning. It means holding onto your past.

You see, the fracturing of God as encumbrances is only locked up in the past. That is where it is locked up. You are the

122

victims of your past experiences. A chronic one in this audience is that you have been abused by your parents, or you were ignored or abandoned by your parents, that you move through life with this sickening attitude of lack. You point the finger at them, or him or her — these are examples — or to your friend or someone who abused you, or to someone who took advantage of you, or someone who pulled the rug out from under you. You go through life pointing fingers. "It is their fault I am this way." That is the fracturing of self. What that means is that instead of taking responsibility for creating this — which is what God is about, God is the creator and that is what you are — instead of taking the responsibility of that, which will define self, you fracture it by pointing fingers and saying, "They did this to me and I was innocent." No one is innocent. The moment that you do this and create tyrants in your life, then you have taken part of the temple and set it in that place, and its reality and its dynamic are to do this to you.

It is so tempting from the human point of view to be a victim, because everyone is. That is the social consciousness of capitalism, to be victimized so that they can find ways to get you out of it temporarily. It is much easier to say I am the way I am because of this and that — people, places, things, times, and events. And when you do, it works for a while. Look how you have used it. You have used it to excuse your lack of strength. You have used it to excuse your illness. You have used it to cleverly bind people to you through their sympathy and empathy. You have used it to get your way. It has served you. You are a capitalist. That is what you are. No one really wants to give that up because the animal in you — the survivalist with definable boundaries, the herdlike creature — that creature demands survival. If every one of you stopped serving the herd, what happens is that the moment you say "I created it" — "I" is God — "I created it, this is my own creation," you remove your power from your parents, people, places, things, times, and events. You remove it from those and start to rebuild the temple within. Now that is a very painful process.

The dark night of the soul is when we finally take responsibility for our actions. What happens then is that the energy that is coming home from poor mom and dad — the energy coming home from your brother, sister, husbandman, wife, or your relationship — when you start to take responsibility, look how consciousness works. If consciousness has control of energy, when you take "I" from out there and put it back within, then the energy starts to dissolve from mom and dad and starts moving back to you. It is passing through those bands and it is coming home.

The dark night of the soul is when the energy rushes through the emotional body. In other words, it was once sent out through the emotional body as feeling to create. It is going to come back home and impact the same feeling. Only when energy becomes purified is when it enters back into the physical realm of the emotional body. Simply said, when you take your power back of making someone else your tyrant, then the energy starts coming back to you in the form of a tyrant. That energy is a thought-form. It is tyrannical, and it hits the emotional body and is like a reverse charge. Instead of the energy coming from within and being affected hormonally, it is coming from out there, passing through the energy band and hitting the body as a direct charge. It is a reverse charge into the brain. When it does, it activates the field and causes suffering. This is where tears, wailing, and anguish come from. If someone says to you, "What is wrong with you?" and you reply, "I don't know," this is what it is. Your chickens are coming home to roost.

Now this is very hard to do. I have taught you so much to

have joy and I will continue to teach you to do that, but you must be free of your encumbrances. What you started, you must complete and bring the energy back to the temple within. You have to build it within yourself. That is redefining it, and it is painful. No one wants to take responsibility for something that all these years has served them so well. They don't want to take responsibility that really they are the one that lived in the past of a circumstance and that the people who were connected have long gone. Nobody wants to admit that this is how they lived their life. It is hard.

When energy passes through the dark night of the soul, then it is home and the self starts to be defined. This is pure judgment, and I will tell you something that will become self-evident: The spiritual path is the path of purging and it is the path of cleansing. It is nothing about cleansing the body or the colon. It is not that. I am not speaking in those terms. I have to be very clear.

Energy between two points of consciousness is defining time, its velocity, its momentum. It is defining time. Now you have two levels of consciousness in this body. You have body/mind consciousness, you have God consciousness, and therefore time bounces back and forth between the two. But if we take that and understand it as a momentum, the body is continuously under emotional duress. This means that if it is, the emotions that are moving from within the body are draining the storehouses of hormones and energy that govern them. Those fundamental building blocks of the tangible physical are being used up every day by reminding yourself of something that you used to get away with in your youth but has taken its toll in middle age. Every day the emotional trauma of your past eats away, and that is time. That is why when the encumbrances of the past are owned and the power is taken back, the past reaction ceases. All ascension becomes then is the natural apogee from owning one's encumbrances. The master truly is walking on the face of the Earth at this point.

The true spiritual life is about a life that you are born into to understand self and heal it and make a life dedicated to the art of healing it. What begins to happen that is so different than the group across the river that is inventing computers is that the spiritual life is an eternal one so that when you do heal it, you belong to the ages and you belong to eternity. When you focus on what has given you life and what you truly are — endeavor to become it, understand its methodology and science and the mechanics of how it works — when you dedicate a life to doing that, then that Spirit is your reward in a never-ending existence.

Now this school is defining that self, defining it. You only make it hard on yourselves. Isn't that an interesting phrase, hard on self? It takes on a new light, does it not? In the orientation about going to the light and the Day of Judgment, you learned about being all things in that light review, the subject as well as the Observer. You learned that after you have this light review, as troubling as it is, you are nonetheless closer to your natural element on Bliss than you are here in this foreign land, and therein you have a place to which you can go into contemplation. You learned about the different areas of contemplation, from pizza parlors on the fourth plane, sitting by a great and beautiful placid lake — it instantly appears — sitting in the midst of the Void somewhere. We call it the halls of contemplation — now this is important — in which we have the ability of contemplation. You have now been removed out of your altered ego.

You can retain the likeness of your former body, if you wish, to help remind you what you need to do, but you have been removed from it. You don't really care who you left behind anymore. You don't really care about what went on with your personal property after your death. You really don't care. As much as the lawyers tell you, you don't care. You really are very different than what you were in that human existence, but you are close to the existence. You have to now go and, taken from what you gained from that existence, have to be able to contemplate — knowing that contemplation is your natural order — because as soon as you do, it appears. You must contemplate on how to finish the business that in yet another lifetime you were unable to do.

You all know when you are in that place how cowardly the body is, the human is. You know that. How do you yet move into that orb of experience and be able to impress what you want upon a brain that clearly is not going to remember? As long as you understand the unity, God is one, then the sweet things of your life are going to be carried on genetically. If you bore children in that life, then one honorable thing that will happen is that you have started a bloodline to which you helped produce, and here is the advantage of that. You know that your attitudes become flesh in the next generation, and what better place would you want to land and work on unfinished business but in the very genetic pool that you are endeavoring to address concurrently.

In this place you are endeavoring to figure out that line of potential and create your future, to be able to finish up this business. Again, let me tell you it is not about being a good person or a bad person. It is about what you do with opportunities and with which level of consciousness do you approach them. Do you approach them with the human that is instinctively a coward or with the Spirit that is all-prevailing? It is about creating, experiencing, so that the soul has yet another block, another tool, to build another reality based upon that wisdom. That is why it is so important.

You know all of this, but you know that your unfinished business can never be finished on Bliss. Oh, you can see the end of it. Why, you can see what you are in other realms. You get the opportunity to play there. You get the opportunity to instantly see what you would be if you were this life or that life or some other life. You are only limited to what you know, and you get to do all of that. You can take your next incarnation and go all the way through. You can visualize for yourself the most idealistic life, but it isn't really going to happen for you. You are not going to gain the substance of the wisdom unless you come back to the place of its origin, down here, the plane of demonstration — the thick, gooey, syrupy plane. This is where you have to be defined and you have to make it known here.

How do you transfer your sublime and sparkling consciousness that immediately imagines and it is? How can you get that magic into that body? Well, you know that the only way you can get it there is if you lay a course ahead of time on Bliss of what you want to have accomplished down here. Now how are you going to get into it? You are going to permeate the bands that surround the tissue of the child in the womb. The child in the womb is going to feed off of those bands. But, more importantly, you have laid the program in the soul, the one who remembers. And the soul is what is going to give life to the child in utero. The soul is going to create the rhythmic beating of the heart. It also, because it is called the lord of the body, has jurisdiction over how the genes play a part in manufacturing the body. It is going to do that. But it is not going to make the brain have memory of which it does not yet have. It can only store it away in the lower cerebellum. That is the only place it is allowed to store it. You know that when you are on Bliss.

What is being a spiritual person about? It is about being the self utterly and totally, that self is all things and all beings.

If who you want to be is spiritual, the self will never, ever hold a grudge against anyone. If you don't do it on Bliss and you have instantaneous manifestation, why do you insist on doing it here? And, second, you should forgive everyone, because in doing so you forgive yourself. In forgiving yourself, you take the monkey off of your back and give the power back to you. When you learn that everyone is you in the way that you are, then you are being spiritual. Why can you not be on Earth as you are in heaven? You simply have to choose to be it and look at the conditions of being it. If there is no cheating in heaven, why do you do it here? If there is no doubting in heaven, why do you insist on doing it here? If there is no malice in heaven, why do you insist on doing it here?

Let's have a toast to more freedom. Isn't it so that the truth does set you free? It does.

God,
let us always wish
for that freedom.
So be it.
To life.

Resolution, a Spiritual Revolution

The next point that we learned was resolution — resolution — a very nice word. It sounds like revolution, a spiritual revolt. We have already discussed what unfinished business is. Although I have put out some very harsh examples, it is an irony that those are the examples that are always put forward because, as I have said to you, there are things about your life that will always be with you. They are the sweet things, the true Godhead. Those are the great acts that you do that really transcend the normal course of business. There are aspects of yourself that you have earned the right by which to be defined. These aspects, as in human consciousness, you could say are the good things. They are the virtuous things, the virtuous lessons, the virtuous deeds. Now there are things about all of you — aspects, colors, dimensions — that are really quite spectacular and you have earned the right to keep those. Those are not disingenuous to your nature. They are quite genuine. Those we don't need to talk about. When you do acts, when you impart the extraordinary from yourself, you are not fracturing; you are defining. And those qualities all of you have.

Everyone in this school at some point in your life has been called upon by a friend or a desperate neighbor, or in a time of chaos and misery, and something greater has risen out of you and you have acquiesced. Now these are the great, defining qualities in your lives that will never be taken away from you because they echo what God is. And you know, my beloved people, there are certainly many incidents in nature or through intentional human destruction in which all of you have been participants. Whereas only days before you may have been griping and complaining about your neighbors, isn't it interesting how the humanity part of you is quick to recognize that in someone else because that is what is in you. That is where your energy is. That is the fracturing of yourself. And then the next day a terrible incident could befall those neighbors perhaps in a very life-threatening way and suddenly, without even thinking, you are riveted from your comfort zone of conceit and arrogance and are transported into a venue of thought that seems to spring from somewhere deep inside of you and you rush to their aid and help. You hold back the waters, you move the food. You take raggedy, smelly children in your arms and where two days before you couldn't tolerate the sight of blood, you are there cleaning wounds, holding them dear to your breast where your soul lives, and you are helping. When two days before you were complaining about your lack of revenue or lack of funds, suddenly it doesn't even become an issue. Your hand reaches for your pocketbook and you pull it out and give, and you don't even think about the consequences of giving.

Now that is your nature, your true, defining moments of self. When you do help, no matter the cost — and sometimes the greater the call, the greater the cost, the greater the effort — it is in those moments that you are defined as God. You truly are. As some historians would say, those are the defining moments, the crowning jewel of human existence. These are the great points about you. There is not one of you that really hasn't, in a small or large way, riveted from the hypocrite to the God in a matter of moments. When you do those kindnesses, that thoughtfulness, those areas of generosity without thought of the repercussion to yourself, you are God. When you pause and reflect and think, then you redefine your boundaries and the moment passes, and that defining of God has missed its opportunity.

This act of emergency that you arise to is what helps to not only define the self but also binds you to the eternal self. Now these are the great things that you have done. Someone who loses their purse in which they have all of their life savings, and you who are working on fabulous wealth find it, it is a great temptation to say that it is your manifestation. That is the altered human instinct to survive. The honorable God, without question, would find its rightful owner. In that rarefied moment you are back on the Plane of Bliss because on the Plane of Bliss there is no need. There is only the expansion of knowledge to make greater forms of preexistence. That is when the God kicks in. That is when you are at your best. That is when you are most ennobled.

How many opportunities are you placed in where the living truth of the Spirit is able to speak instead of the cunning of the flesh? You are in them every day. How many opportunities are there for you to shine nobly what you are when it would be easier to hide and become pale and run away? You have all done this, and this is your beauty. This you will never have to be ashamed of in the light of all eternity. It is not something that you have to own in this lifetime. It is the fabric of the construction of self, and you all have that to your credit. It takes a truly remarkable man and woman to be in the fire of social consciousness and suddenly, in a blinding moment, know the right path and take it.

Resolution is taking those splendid moments to your credit and applying them in the areas that you are encumbered in and not apply them with human logic — because human logic will always have an ulterior motive — but apply those splendid moments forthrightly from that which is termed the spiritual self that created them somewhere else.

I tell you it is a finer thing to walk away from the emotions that rip and tear you apart. It is a finer being who can get up off of their knees and dust themselves off and walk away. They may have nothing when they do, but they are finer, more ennobled, and more spiritual in that moment than in the fray of who is right and who is wrong. It takes a very powerful person to do that, but those are the acts that give us this defining quality of God.

You chose the spiritual learning. That is why you are here. I set up the format. You chose to be here to learn about that which is not completely tangible. You learned in this life to help define you instead of living in the fog of life after life which on that plane, before you were incarnated, all of you found a central core of something that needed to be done. You needed to study. You needed to define what it was that has been forgotten instead of going over those same meaningless experiences and never finding resolution to them. You chose in heaven a part of your linear process to be here, and if you hadn't, you wouldn't be in this school.

There are no victims in this audience to the spiritual teaching. It is here by design and by choice. You are following your soul's journey. What higher life could anyone live than to live the life that defines God, because ultimately that is what everything is. You chose to be here in this learning. And, remember, you obviously thought that I knew what I would be talking about and that it was important enough for you to tarry with me for a time and dedicate a part of your life to gaining this. In that potential you created, you saw its value, of course, and you remembered the different road I took than the one you have taken ever since. You remembered that, and you are here then to be dedicated to the knowledge that I am giving you and to teach you how to think, not as a fractured God but one that is whole, and to keep showing you through processes which, though very difficult, can be very simple. You chose to be here.

The spiritual Godhead is the resolution to everything because it is in it that when you learn about self, then self is no longer cloaked in mystery. Although it is much bigger and broader than any painting that you could put forth, you still begin to have a sense of its presence. You begin to study your tracks and begin to look at the tracks that you have made. When you do, you will be closing in on the invisible presence that has made them, and you are here to know that. When you do, you will find all of the answers that resolve the encumbrances with which you are all dealing. You have heavy ones that you obviously haven't been able to get out of and so you have gone to the fountainhead itself on this plane to find your way out and be free of them.

How then do we resolve? Resolution is so simple it can happen in a moment. It is the same moment of clarity that happens when you finally give up your past and lay that focus in clear water, and then it happens. It is a dynamic showing you that all you must do is be able to move above your past and no longer affiliate with it. You must do the work as the human to forgive in every quarter so that you can find forgiveness, because only then are you forgiven. It must come from you. To do it out here gives permission for the God or the prodigal son to come home, and the tears of joy are passing through that emotional barrier. At every area in your life you must look to see what bothers you, what infringes upon your peace, what drives you and who drives you, and why you keep thinking in terms of the past rather than the present. You must get rid of it by taking your energy off of it. When you do, you become whole.

That is not to say that the drama of tangible reality doesn't continue to play; it does for a while. This then brings into full forbearance the teaching of looking at the table and seeing it filled, even though it appears to the eye to be empty. Forgive, forgive, forgive, forgive, forgive; release, release, release, release; allow, allow, allow, allow. At every act of the way you become empowered. Remember, you want it all back, and it is locked up in the past. You want it all back.

Now here is the frightful moment of doing that. When you do that, you sometimes cut the lifeline to your own sovereignty. In other words, your sovereignty, your boundaries, your definition of love and companionship are all based in these places you are about to cut out from under you. You are literally pulling the rug out from under your carnal life. Well, that is what the spiritual journey is about. You want to do that. You want to take the box and shake it up and throw it out there. Yes, you are going to fall on your face. Yes, everything ceases for a while. Yes, it is going to happen. What else do you expect? "Well, the cupboard is empty but I am empowered." Yes, yes, you are. But if you even dare to regret that the cupboard is empty, you are not empowered. Isn't regret also an empowerment of the Godhead? You have to stop regretting. There cannot be any regrets, none, because if you do, you are fractured. And what you want is not to save face but to become empowered again.

In the sense of the term that I have talked about, that makes you naked and vulnerable, it seems, and you get the shakes and are nervous. But if you can hold that pure place, it is the same place that happens when you break down and finally tell the truth to that fool. You know, you don't even care any longer what the repercussions are. It can't be any worse than what you have been experiencing, and when it is finally done, you feel so light. You don't care if the house falls down around you, you feel light. That is spiritual — that is the Spirit — and the Spirit is starting to float. It is coming together again, and that is where the training on how to start applying pure power to what you are doing starts to become so important.

When you have resolution and get to work on this in your life, how is the best way to work at it? You have to stay conscious. You can work eight hours of the day unconscious but let's dedicate at least two hours of the day being conscious, being so conscious and so aware that you really influence the other eight hours. How many of you understand that you really do make an impact? In those conscious moments I train you how to first release the energy from the first three seals, which is the grounding place here. It is the first discipline you ever learn to do in my school, to pull that energy up. I teach you the discipline of Consciousness & Energy® and it is proved by science that it works. I teach you to do that. First you have to get out — out — of this plane and you have to be able to become mobile in the Spirit. You have to take the energy out of these places and it has to come up here to the head, and that is what C&E® does. If it is up here, you can shoot on into the Void, and you should go there. You should allow yourselves to dissolve into nothing — into nothing. Remember, consciousness and energy is creating reality. This is your natural place, Bliss. You are imagination. It is a product of you. You have to go home to your natural self, your productivity of imagination, and the Void is where you dip into to be cleansed, purified, and free of your attachment. When you are ready and unattached, then you can move from the Void back into Point Zero again. You move then from nothing into God — from nothing to God — and then from God you are at the pinnacle of your spiritual self. How long does this take? It is dependent upon the master. Some of you in an hour of blowing, you still won't get there; others of you in two breaths, you are there. There is no standard. It is all individual. It all means how deep are you ingrained in the first three seals and do you want to get out of them. Some people don't like to get out of them. Some people want to feel tired in the mornings and they want to feel this and want to feel that, so wherever their want is, is where they are.

The closer you are working in the spiritual and that becomes your prerequisite, then you want to wash yourself of this body. You want to go take a swim in nothing and then come back to the Godhead absolutely pure. You are at the spiritual head. You are now in the Observer's point of view. You are getting now to take a look. As you start to fall from Point Zero and fall into the fifth, fourth, and third levels — which you are going to do when you start imagining — you are going to come back to a very familiar place. This is the place from where you created the opportunities in this life and you are going to fall into them. They are going to become very familiar. You are going to fall into those, and as the Observer you are going to allow the review of this life and what you want to accomplish to pass before you. The line of potential has already been set up for you to do so. It is easy to do.

What do you want to work on? You want to become unencumbered of your regret. Today it is regret and it will just come on you. What you are to do is you take regret and you blow it out three times in C&E® until it is clear. You will know when you have effected it because there will be an incredible beingness of lightness in the fourth seal. What is then going to happen is all of the people, places, things, times, and events that regret is attached to will start to pass in front of you, and each one of them you do the same thing. You address it. You are now consciously addressing it. Or it may be forgiveness. Remember, I told you that you can tell who you have run into from the Plane of Bliss. Who you have made a deal with is going to be the most difficult person to forgive, and that is someone that agreed to play that part for both you and for them. You are going to have to root it out and find them and you are going to have to address it. When it comes to your parents — a most precarious relationship — you can no longer sit as judge over another person's actions. So far in being the victim, you have been their tormentor. You can no longer sit in that place of power to hold them responsible and blame them for everything in your life. You are going to have to set them free, because only in doing that do you get the power back that is no longer rooted in blame. Then you are free — my God, you are free — and you can feel it as it starts to wash you.

You may spend the next six months doing that same process until one day it is a no-thing. You will wake up in the morning, you will look out that window, and it is not there anymore. God, be it that you are so empowered. The moment you decide to do this is when you start the true, spiritual path because it means that you are reaching for a higher and loftier order to reframe from the lower order of yourself.

Now that is the means and how you are going to get it accomplished. The sticky part is you can take care of superfluous things that really aren't deep in your core. You have to reach down and find those issues we talked about, that when you face the fracturing of your God and heal it now, there will be nothing to look at in the light to come, and with that you begin to see that self becomes more identifiable. It is really a God that once it is freed up from its encumbrances and its burdens of finishing up its creations, look what is standing in front of it that has an enormous wealth and revenue of reality to bring forth. And because it is not cluttered, it brings it forth quickly, not in a long period of wait.

The only reason you haven't gotten everything that you want is because you have too many things standing in the way. What you want is the future. What stands in the way is the past. How could you possibly make room for the future when you don't have any because it is cluttered by the past? And simply wanting it isn't enough. There has to be power to instigate it, power to imagine. How can you possibly imagine an unimaginable when your thoughts are always riveted to some little, emotional trauma that you are feeling? You are not going to imagine the unimaginable if you are thinking about food. You are not going to imagine the unimaginable if you are sitting there suffering, if you are sitting there regretting, wishing you could be someplace else. There is no room for it. There is no God for that to happen, so it won't work. That is why it is important that you do this by sheer choice because then you give yourself enough power to follow through with what you are learning. You never, ever have follow-through if you don't want to be here. Runners don't come; nothing happens. You have to be open for it. In resolution you become clear of your past and it is no longer there and you don't have energy on it. The master hunts it down, digs it out, roots it out, confronts it, and confronts it for the sake of self.

It is really incidental what anyone else does. If you have made the move to retrieve back your energy, if you forgive them of something they can't quite let go of, then the rubber band bounces back in their face and the energy from it comes back to you. Then it is their issue. It has nothing to do with you anymore. The way you will know is that no matter how much they try, they won't arouse a response because there is nothing there to arouse. It is as if the incident never happened.

Now this makes for an interesting day when we continue to have resolution. It should be your focus, because what are you going to talk about then? What do you have to talk about? It is the same thing about what do you bring to the table to a master. Why do you think that you deserve to be in their presence? You don't, any more than what do you have to talk about if you have resolved the past with someone, someplace, something, some event? What do you have to talk about? There is nothing to talk about and that is when you know you are free of it. You don't have to have an appointment to go back and rehash it. Sometimes people just like to dig up the past because it takes them out of the present backwards and they think they have to do that. There is nothing to talk about and that is when you know it is finished.

Why linger there any more than a master would want to sit there and talk about you to you? Why should they want to do that? It is the same analogy. Isn't that what you want to be? Then why do you want or have the need to go back and have a conversation if the conversation was always based upon the dynamics of regret, resentment, failure, heartbreak, loss — and we could put that in all kinds of categories — jealousy, envy, betrayal, all of that. If you have resolved that in yourself and there is nothing to talk about, what kind of conversation are you then going to have? Are you going to try to regurgitate it and get it back up there and start working it back up in a frenzy so that you have an equal playing field? Cut its head off.

This is called enlightenment. You begin to see why you have grinding relationships. They grind on you. You know why? Because it is over with and the only meeting ground that you have is to meet on those conditions. You don't know when to leave. You are a little confused on obligation here. You don't know when to give it up because the only thing it is giving you is this friction. You have grown. You don't fit anymore. Do you understand? That is when you walk away because that part has been played and it should be finished. Now what does that do? Is your human intelligence going to tell me that this means you just kick your friends out? They are not a friend. They are a God. You have no beholding to any God but giving them freedom. That is the way it is.

True friendship doesn't grind; it grows together. It is Gods growing in ultimate freedom together. There is no grind there. That is why I tell you there is no lack in it. So why are you going to go back and keep rehashing it? Is that the only premise that you can meet equally upon? Tell me, my beloved people, is that resolution? No, that is regeneration of fracturing. That is what that is. You must walk away. You have nothing to talk about. Think about the basis of your conversations every day. What are they based on? It depends upon the person, the place, the thing, and the event, doesn't it? Well, why revisit it? It is over with.

Now there is grace in that. Isn't it grace to have a community of individuals as family but that in that greater, spiritual family there is no dominion, there is no agreeance in that family to meet on the conditions of any past, and that the family are each individual Gods? There are forests of them that are growing, and as the energy grows and changes in one, it is spread to everyone else. That is what we want.

You are confused about friendship. You made friends in paradise. You made friends only because they became closely associated with you in your journey here in integral parts and you have met them along the way all through your lives. You have yet to meet many more who just wait for their part they are going to play in the potential that is yet to be unfolded, when the self has been healed. They are yet to come too.

In God we are one. You don't have to make that clear delineation. When you helped your neighbor, you didn't think whether they were your friend or not. You helped them because it was something urgent in you that did it. That is the sort of relationship I am talking about.

Practical Application and Instructions from Ramtha

I have a list here of four things: free will and choice, defining self, unfinished business, and resolution. I want you to take each of these four things and separately image them. For example, resolution is going to be a little difficult. I want you to draw pictures of them. I want you to draw a choice to be here. What does that look like to you? What do free will and choice look like? If you have to think about that, then you are going to have a new definition on its meaning, its performance.

Defining self, how do we draw self? One of the most endearing symbols, of course, is we can use the blue star. But I like the heart because God is love and the heart also sits by the fourth seal. What if we start out with the premise that the self is a heart. Let's begin with that concept and then let's tear it apart. Let's fracture it, break it down, and move bits and pieces of it over here to demonstrate that a piece of my heart, a piece of my God, is empowering my victimization or my tyranny or my greed or over here something else. Then it is up to you to meticulously create your past and where your energy is locked up, and don't leave anything out. Take a piece of the heart to show that the only reason that past is in place is because it has been sanctioned by divine energy.

If we can show that effectively on a drawing, we get a great visual — inspired by the master and followed through by the student on a great, profound teaching — that if you can put it into a picture and draw it, it will be one of the greatest mandalas you will ever do because it is yours. It is real and it is about you and your journey. We then make another drawing on defining it. Defining it is going to encompass these two aspects: First you have to get the energy back, so you start to see in picture after picture what you must do to bring your heart back and put it where it is now perfect again. You have to see measure by measure what you must do to get your energy back, and you must draw those pictures of it.

Those pictures are going to also include number three, unfinished business, because the unfinished business is the encumbered self. It is the past self, the past unfinished, and you are going to have to draw pictures of those. What is unfinished? What have you started that you are in the midst of and can't get out? Where are you still human and where are you not God? What seems to be your great learnings in this life? Where are your weaknesses? That will point to the unfinished business and the encumbered self. I want you to draw not a caricature of some fictional entity but a caricature of yourselves and what lies unfinished. However you depict that, it is going to be all right, and then I want you to draw resolution. Perhaps the greatest way to draw resolution is to redraw the heart. Radiant and shining inside of an undersized body, there is an oversized heart that talks about a place of spiritual peace. Or perhaps you can draw the body and mimic it as the temple and that shining through its spires and its windows is the radiant light of spiritual power. Perhaps that is how you see it. Or perhaps you see resolution as the rolling up of some ancient scroll long left undone and seeing it rolling up. Or maybe you see then a cage opening and the flight of a dove. However you picture it, it must be a picture that is meaningful to you. When you do it correctly, then you will understand your own journey. Mandalas should not be made en masse. They are personalized aspects of one's own journey. They should be created by you.

It is important for the master to be a master but not an intimidating one. It is important for the master — whose greatest phenomenon will be the endless show of wisdom, which is the gift of the master — not to intimidate but to encourage. I tell you, I do so ask that you feel encouraged by what you have learned today and that you feel you are in a place that is safe enough for you to address this and safe enough to be encouraged to want to change. I tell you, you are never going to disappoint me. Oh, I have left these events and at moments had to go refigure my dream, keep downsizing it, but you are never going to disappoint me because I am not at a place that I could ever be disappointed, thank God. And so with that, you see, you have the freedom to be yourselves, the freedom to go and change, and my love is not going to change for you. It does not float in and out on the tide. It is not fickle. I love you. I desire that you feel comfortable enough to be inspired by who I am and what I am, even though you can't see me, because that is the kingdom of the Spirit. That is what is radiating out here in front of you that is so beautiful, and perhaps in this ideal you will want it enough to be impassioned enough to take a stand and do it. I want to give you the room to do that. I just thought I should tell you that. So be it.

If you are utterly self-empowered, what anyone says about you will never move you from your center and it won't fracture you. That then is just a state of radiating love. When you can still love and bless them for their opinion, then you are a true kindred of the highest order, but you should not move down to their level for the sake of kindredship. You have to bloom in their midst in spite of them and for them. I promise you that one sweet hour they will call upon you and you will have the power in their need to do marvelous things. Therein lies the gift of being your own master.

I expect for you to apply diligently what you have learned here because it is given from a greater and more priceless place than this place that you know. Use it. If you don't, you have nothing to complain about when your life, instead of getting greater as a result of the teachings, seems to become diminished by them. So be it. Be happy. I love you.

O my beloved God,
I awaken to your presence
in the present.
O my beloved God,
deliver me from my past
and reclaim my kingdom.
O my beloved God,
bring forward in me
the great virtues
that I shall deserve.
O my beloved God,
God bless my body
and change my life.
So be it.
To life.

CHAPTER 6
DEATH AND THE REVELATION OF
OUR ULTERIOR MOTIVE

*"The ulterior motive — ulterior, the real motive
behind the action — now that is where you are
judged ... The only way you are ever going to be
released from the plane of Terra and the human
experience is to conquer it. How do you conquer
it? By the revelation of your ulterior motive and the
degrees of prejudice in which you use it.
That tells the whole story."*

— Ramtha

Revelation of Our Ulterior Motive

O my beloved God,
manifest straightaway
my created day
and let me marvel
at my simple power.
So be it.
To life.

The Plane of Bliss is that marvelous, golden place that I taught you about where you go after passing from the physical body, if you are fortunate enough to go on — some don't go on — that after going to the light and being stripped, you then see everything from your conception in the womb to the day you passed. Remember, all actions are the direct result of conscious intent. The action is actually the energy of conscious intent, so it becomes a living, viable concept through action, energy. When I tell you that consciousness and energy are inextricably combined, it is a truth, because in what you do is the action of what you know, and we call that doing "the experience of reality."

All of those experiences are logged in your brain and in those bands that surround your body. Those bands that surround your body are governed by the soul. It is the soul in a light review that gives up her knowledge. In other words, the Book of Life is opened, and in opening the Book of Life one sees what we cannot talk about in reference to linear time, but we must say that the time that it takes to see this is a brief moment, yet a million years. When you review this life lived here you are both the Observer, the participant, and the receiver, which is

148

interesting, because that statement goes back to say that we are all things in our reality, including all people. Those people and our affection — indeed that which is termed our magnetism to them — are aspects of them that we are. That is where we are bound with them. Just as things in our reality are reflections of us, where we are is a reflection of our reality. Everything around us is really the action of the thoughts that we have being realized. Human beings have a problem because they see the thoughts in their life as something separate from what they are doing. They see themselves separate from the things in their life. They see themselves separate from the people in their life. In other words, we say that is a fine individual, and that individual is a sovereign God, but the fineness that we see in that individual is equal to the fineness that we are. The reason they are in our life is that they reflect perfectly and exquisitely an aspect of ourselves.

The royal road to perfection is to trash our life of imperfection and fill it only with the highest pinnacle of reflection that we beseech in ourselves. To do otherwise is to live a lie — a hypocritical lie — or a life in which we have prostituted the lofty aspects of ourselves for the common denominator of simply being accepted, or the common denominator of survival, which is certainly the human drama lived in the first three seals of sexual activity, birth, pain, power, and victimization. If we seduce our lives to live here and abash our loftiness, then we are going to see exactly what that is in a light review. A master trashes his or her life and gets rid of the dross, the imperfect. It gets rid of the seduction, gets rid of the lie, the hypocrisy, the victimization, the tyranny, gets rid of all of it. A master puts in its life — if only one bright and beautiful thing — that one bright and beautiful thing that mirrors exquisitely the apex of the master's ability to perform reality, that it is exactly what it is up here in your brain.

149

Now you are all simply learning to do that. That is what change is about — change in the context that it is fruitful, letting your life fall apart and letting go of the dross, the heaviness, working too hard to keep something together that does not bring joy, but only when you glue it together does it form a crack in your reality.

Coming back to the light review, in a light review what becomes exquisite is the way the soul plays it out in energy. The drama is more than three dimensions. It is actually seven dimensions because you are seeing it from the Godhead, which is every player in the drama. You are seeing it from the Observer, which is the Spirit in the drama, and you are seeing it from the soul's perception, which is the personality/individual in the drama who thinks it is an individual. You are seeing it from a holy place on all levels, and what begins to happen then is the whole life starts to play out in front of you. Every thought creates an action. You become the thought. You as personality feel the action but as the Godhead, as the Spirit, you are the reaction of that action to the whole environment so you are experiencing it on every level. Isn't this where true learning is, to actually know what our thoughts and actions do to others, other lifeforms?

This is a painful process, but the God in you holds you steady with love and keeps all of the multifaceted vision in place so that you don't break down and weep and get caught up in your individuality, which begins to see the drama it has created. It sees the suffering that it has created in another individual, in another lifeform. It sees the difficulty in the environment that it has caused for its selfish reasons because it wants to be acknowledged as an individual. It sees its power and how that power warps and bends, and the God that is so loving keeps all of your perspective together. It keeps the Spirit intact at this review, keeps the soul intact, which is the personality in this review, and the God. They all stay together.

In one moment you weep and can hardly bear to see what you are looking at, but then the love of God that is all things flows right to you and gives you the strength to continue to view from different reflections. Otherwise, you would never make it through because it is enough in this life that you have created such regret. It is going to be a very difficult problem in the light review to see your intentions on others, the environment, lifeforms. And, subsequently, who is ultimately crippled? You are. Every one of you has had this happen before and you are going to have it happen again.

Once you get this well-rounded of what the great self really is, you really are something much more extraordinary than the isolated human being that you think you are. You are really more. Remember what I told you that makes great initiates. This individual body that seems so isolated is only a splinter of what you really are, because the great self is ultimately everything.

There are people who take that teaching and prostitute it in a very fanatical and unfortunate way — all is the one and the one is the all — which is philosophy that has not been actualized except to a point that it is self-serving. If it is self-serving, it is actualized. If it isn't, it remains philosophical. In other words, people toy with a spiritual life because it is advantageous to them at certain times. It gives them an advantage rather than a stability which is the bread of their life by which they live. They have to have a greater understanding than that. At the light you begin to see how your intentions are profoundly affected in everyone and how, if you have ulterior motives in any of your actions, always those ulterior motives are the overlying and underlying crime.

The ulterior motive — ulterior, the real motive behind the action — now that is where you are judged. You are never judged on the surface. You are judged and weighed by your ulterior motive — ulterior. That is why being impeccable is such an important charge to the student. Be impeccable. Do not have an ulterior motive. If you do, get rid of all the window dressing and take a look at it. That is what you must refine, not the window dressing but the ulterior motive behind your actions. Being impeccable is living from that ulterior place because that is the engine of your life and it is the engine behind everything that you do.

How common is this? Here is a common example: being nice to someone, exceptionally kind to someone, and it isn't for the sake of kindness; it has an ulterior motive to it. Now all of you have done that. The ulterior motive is that you are wanting something from that person, you are, whether it is a relationship on any of the levels or whether it gives you something. Usually the ulterior motive is what you really want, and you use kindness as the chariot in which to get it. It is the ulterior motive in you that you must refine. You must refine it and it must be refined without emotion. In other words, it has already got an emotional attachment to it. To become its emotion then is to become it again. You must refine it without people, places, things, times, and events. When you do that, you have changed the substance of your being. Now you become an impeccable person. You do exactly as your ulterior motive says. You are your ulterior motive. There are no confusing signals out here. You are what you are.

The complication in a light review is that the ulterior motive is what you as a personality get to experience. The deception is what you experience as the object of your ulterior motive, the deception being the unimpeccable intention. In other words, you simply get to be the person that you are being kind to, that you get bottlenecked into giving something away, that you feel used, feel betrayed, or you were a pawn in a game. When you gave of yourself through true kindness, you realized that you were moved as a pawn to get something from you, that the kindness was disingenuous. You get to experience that betrayal of a disingenuous move. How is it that you can understand that? Because there have been many of you that have been on that receiving side of a disingenuous person who gives you what you want in order to get something from you.

We can get very basic with this and talk about the power of women over men. Women have an absolute power over men because they rule a man's loins. They do, make no mistake about it, and that is their power. Is it love? No, it is seduction. Well, what is seduction? An ulterior motive for something else, that the activity is given as a power to submit the male energy to a governing force that has a whole different agenda. Now this is where you get to see it in its rawest, most animallike nature, and you see the abuse of it. You see the ignorance of man — the ignorance and stupidity of man for his loins — that his brain is really in his penis, and you see a powerful and skillful operator, a femme fatale. In the light you get to be all of that and know what it is to be used.

You see, we can take that example then to levels of pain and suffering — pain and suffering. A suffering person has power over a well person. A powerful person — a demonstrative, powerful person — has charge over lesser people. That is why you have principalities and kingships and states and countries and local communities. Politicians have power over the people. It is the same seduction as you go back to men and women. And for what? Because a man has an instinct. Instinct is that evolution from the sensitivity of original polarization. You are sensitive to what you are not. You are sensitive to what you are not because when you get it, you become whole, and in wholeness you bear the children. You do not bear children out of unwholeness. In nature the law is very simple. You are

attracted to what you are not, and when you come together with
that which you are not, you form a unity of oneness. In oneness
you have no polarization. When you have no polarization in
oneness, you have analogical mind. In analogical mind, the
seed is planted in the womb. That is what the ecstasy of the
experience is all about, that moment that your mind is in such
a convulsion — your nerves have put you into such ecstasy —
that in that moment of orgasmic experience there is no time.
There is only the experience. The experience in and of itself is
a powerful, energetic, analogical experience. That analogical
experience is wholeness, and only from that brings forth the
child in the womb by natural law.

Why are men suckers? Because they are sensitive to what
they are not, and their serpent power is awesome in their member
because their sensitivity has led to an instinct that propagates the
species. Men, at the bottom of their motives, have an instinct to
propagate. That instinct to propagate is to propagate women in
season to bring about more children. It is a struggle in the base
animal for unity or for God in that moment that propagation
can take place. Here is how you create. The polarities come
together analogically. The idea that collapses into them becomes
reality. That is the highest order, the fountainhead of all nature.
In its basic stratum it comes down to copulation, and that is a
powerful place.

Women are not motivated to the degree in instinct that
men are for orgasmic experience. Their true motivation is not
the orgasmic experience. Their true orgasmic experience is the
powerful surrender of their mate. That is true orgasm. That is
how women see it. Even though women orgasmically can be
fulfilled, their modus operandi, their instinct, is the surrender
of their mate. That is their greatest joy they get. That is why
the oldest profession in the world is still around. That is why

it has been such a success. They never get involved with these people but they know how to bring them to their knees and get what they want out of them. What is it they want? Money, gold, survival, luxury, a way to live.

Now on the Plane of Bliss, whether you are a woman or a man, you are going to see that too. There is no editing of your life. You get to see all those times you were copulating behind the door. You see all the fantasies that you used to do that, because they tell a story of what it takes for you to be submissive. Fantasies warp and warp and warp and warp until finally you have children who are preyed upon because the warping fantasy in the sexual act creates the mental imagery in which orgasmic experience is the rape of innocence. That is why you have predators today — never in my time, but today — who prey upon children because they have fantasized it into being. They weren't born with it; they made it.

This explanation goes back then to ulterior motive. What is the ulterior motive behind every action? When I taught you about the seven seals in the body — the seven levels in the body — and what energy pours out of them, what glands are activated, we can say clearly that the brain lives in those seals.[7] We can see very clearly the hardwiring of an individual because even though the brain is sitting up in the head, it is actually hardwired by these seals and we see so clearly the actions of an individual. And what is their ulterior motive? Their ulterior motive is the energy. That is what they really want. On the Plane of Bliss it is embarrassing to the individual aspect that is viewing it. It is not embarrassing to the Observer, and it is simply reporting the facts by the soul. When you have to observe it, it is going to be embarrassing because the personality/individual of yourself is going to see it. You know

---

7 See "The Seven Seals" and "The Bands" in the Glossary.

your God has been watching the whole time and your soul has been busy — oh, my — and you think, well, this has to get better but you see that the ulterior motive just keeps running through every one of your lives. Every day of your life there is that ulterior motive and you are going, "Oh, my God."

And it is saying, "Yes?"

"This was really me. I thought my life was so adventurous and so fruitful. I thought all those people I had in my life that it was jolly friendship and all of this and all of that. I really thought I had made much more progress."

I don't care who you are. You could have been the king of the world and had all the world as your subjects or you could have been a pauper down on the street of the cheesemakers begging for cheese, and the reality will be the same if every day the same ulterior motive existed. No matter how many people came into your life, how many people left your life, how many things you got, how many things you didn't get, they were all the result of a modus operandi of the personality self, the ulterior motive. And you will say, "My God, I thought I did so much good." Well, wasn't the ulterior motive behind that the same one that you used when you were twenty-two years old? How about when you were seven years old and you thought you were a victim? No, you became a victim and it gave you power. That is the ulterior motive behind that story, so what did you end up with? Every day of your life was just the same-old, same-old, and it is embarrassing. You see that as you start to get older, you get more fanatical and so you get more cunning in ways of control. In other words, you may soften in your old age but has the ulterior motive left? No, because it was never looked at and it was never recognized for all of its equal parts in your life, all that it does, all the drama that it does, all the pain that it inflicts, and all the sickness that comes from it.

The light review is a horrific experience. That is the reason why the great Gods of old that became the priest Pharaohs, their objective in their rule was that at the end of their life their ka and ba could be weighed on the scales of Osiris. Their heart could be placed on one scale and a feather on the other scale and there would be no difference, that the heart, which is intention, is weighed against a feather. Their entire time of rule was very precarious, and yet those who were ruled by them were blessed because they were truly a royal Godhead struggling in a place of power to be the ultimate servant, the ultimate priest, the ultimate governor of people — the ultimate. There is no politician today whose soul could be weighed against a feather. And wouldn't that make a new interesting, political campaign motive? "I will lead you, if you vote for me, in such a way that by the end of this life my intentions will be weighed against a feather." We would all vote for him. Now what does that mean? Without prejudice — prejudice, an important word. You see, there is a lot that goes on in this life review and you begin to see its entanglements in ulterior motives, prejudice.

These beings, which I am endeavoring to teach you to be, in a light review must understand that when you see it, that somewhere along the way it will become obvious that there was needed a meaningful change and the change was not necessarily an environmental change. It had to happen first within the self.

Love yourself and you will be free. What does that mean? That means dig within, find out what is your ulterior motive in degrees of your prejudice. It is very simple. Men are turned on by beautiful women and beautiful women know that. They in fact strive to be that way so in turn they can have the power to have a place, to have commitment, children, survival. If it doesn't work out, they can always gussy up, as it were, and go after someone else — that is their place of power — leaving the poor man holding his member. You laugh because it is the truth. Or it could be the other way around: When the woman has become so comfortable and beauty begins to fade and the man's interest is no longer there, she exchanges it for guilt, children, and your rightful place, and he starts wandering off and looking for new excitement. She is left holding the burdens, but she has the power still. It is called guilt.

He can go out and be submissive all he wants but it is his prejudice that has led him astray inasmuch as it is her prejudice that enticed him, kept him, or let him go. You have to understand the rules of this game, and they are pretty sticky once you get down in here. You see all of that, and it is not a pretty sight. There is not a woman here that is going to be proud to see what she is about to see, and there is not a man here that is going to be proud of what he has to see. That is the reason you come back — that is the reason you come back here — because the only way you are ever going to be released from the plane of Terra and the human experience is to conquer it. How do you conquer it? By the revelation of your ulterior motive and the degrees of prejudice in which you use it. That tells the whole story.

What then do you glean from this very painful, yet most extraordinarily revealing life? Why, the soul is looking at it in sheer fascination. "I can't believe you did all of this." You know when it is over with, the soul is your best buddy.

"I can't believe you did that."

"Well, you kept me up late at night."

"And I kept you up late at night because I kept bothering you right here."

"Oh, yeah, I remember that."

"Well, when are you going to learn? You know, we have been on the same page for all of these days that you had this life. I have written this. I am bored. I have written the same thing down every day."

Once it is over, you get a very clear picture of how primitive you are or how advanced you are, and even the most advanced think they are primitive. That is so beautiful because it is that longing to return to splendid perfection that they come back and they bring back with them gifts of that ennobled existence, and their energy just can't be found in the normal, ulterior-motive realm. They are just somewhere else. They are utterly and totally unique. Now that is the substantive person.

What happens then on the Plane of Bliss? After that exhausting life review you go and get to eat for two or three thousand years anything and everything you want — lots of wine, goat cheese, olives, sweetmeats, turkeys, all of those sorts of things — and then this beautiful kingdom that you get to dwell in is called the Plane of Bliss. It is the golden, beautiful, exquisite plane called paradise. You get to go to school there, and in school you are essentially studying, as it were, the very origins of your difficulty and you study them in a way that the light review showed it to you. You are actually studying the friends that you had on which you perpetrated this and they perpetrated it on you — the lovers you had, the children you had, the family you had — and that is what your school is about. You can never move to a higher school or a greater hall of learning there unless you know how to ask the right question. All you are really doing is learning about the unity of God as a whole, and that God expressed through the individual is impacting the whole of what God is and the greatness of what it is, and you learn that.

Then you go off and have what is called the long season of contemplation, and the long season of contemplation on this beautiful place can be anyplace that is tranquil to your mind. For example, whatever you call tranquillity will appear instantaneously in front of you. To some it will be a tranquil lake, quicksilver ripples on the top reflecting weeping willows and an occasional flower drifting by on a slow, lazy, summer day. Now that is contemplation. There you are going to meet other beings who have the same likeness, and that same likeness is that they manifested the same sort of place and you get to share that with them. If you want absolute solitude, you will get absolute solitude — same place, no visitors. Everything is respected there; nothing is cast out. Or if you see that your place of contemplation is a high mountain place with the great white snow, so it will happen. If your contemplation is riding a great steed in the throes of battle and that is where your energy and your adrenaline are at its greatest, then you get that whole scene.

If your place of contemplation, wherever it is, is around children, then you get to be around little children there. And why are they staying little children? Because that is the place of their greatest innocence where they can contemplate, so they come back to Bliss as little people, little children. They really died perhaps in this experience when they were eighty-two or one hundred and forty or fifty-two years of age or twenty-nine, and yet where do they rest? As a child, and maybe you want to seek their audience. They are learning to be that simple, that when they come back it is their simplicity that overrides everything. In simplicity you do not have ulterior motives; you simply are simple.

Ulterior motive is the thunder passion in your life. That is where your real passion is. That is where your real powerhouse is. When you uncover that, then you have uncovered the great energy storehouse of your life, and when you can bring it to the surface simply, then you can do marvelous things with it.

That is the reason why whenever I address an audience,

you can hear particle dust hit the floor when I talk about sexuality, and everyone has rapt attention — you know that we are looking at ulterior motives here — money, rapt attention, or extraordinary phenomenon, rapt attention. It is the ulterior motives that capture your attention. Isn't it interesting that all three of those are used somewhere on different levels? They absolutely are. The reason that you go to the light is you have to review what fruit did you bear in that life. The only reason you are doing this is to review your progress in making known the unknown and where you are so trapped that you cannot expand.

Freedom from the Deceit of the Past

Your dream is to be free, people — free. That is the ulterior motive. That should be the motive, freedom. Freedom from what? Having to use anyone, any person, place, thing, time, or event, to become it, just to be it. The mastery is to wrestle it out of people, places, things, times, and events because aren't people, places, times, and events what a light review is all about? It absolutely is.

Think about it. This very moment millions of souls are crossing over and getting a light review. There are a lot of fireworks going on somewhere. Millions of them are passing right now. Someone just died a few miles from here. They are gone. They are out of here. They are on their way. Someone else got shot not too far from here in a city, and you know what they are doing? Why, they have just slipped out of their body and they are turning around looking at that phosphorescent skin lying there and they are panicking. You know why? Because that is all they ever thought they were. They are trying to get back in a brain that is no longer firing. They are trying to get back in the body where the blood isn't flowing, and they can't. They are moving in and out of a dead body. It is gone. What are they doing? Their whole modus operandi was a physical life. Why, the reason that they got shot was because it was all about physical dominance. That is what it was about. How enlightened is that soul? It is not very enlightened.

If a woman dies of rape, what kind of fantasies did this woman have? Where did it ultimately lead? What kind of a flirt or an enticer was this woman? What was the ultimate fantasy? Now it is out of its body. What is its worth? What is your worth if you don't have a body? Look at the person you are with. If you didn't have this body and you were in another body, would you still be with them? Think about that, because it is coming. Age and time do that work wonderfully. Excess does that work wonderfully. Think about it. If you look at your partner, the person that you say you love, if they looked any other way could you still love them? If you can't and couldn't, then who are you? Why, you are nothing more than a body. What is going to happen to you? You are going to have a lot of problems.

Remember, not everyone that passes gets a life review. A lot of them are stuck between here and the moon. They are floating around above the ground. They are in the fog. They are in the atmosphere. They are the moon shadows at night. They hang around bars and taverns. They hang around places of excess. They attach to you when you get onto their level. Not everyone gets a life review. Most of them can't find it because their ulterior motive was all about the body. I tell you this because I don't care who you are in this audience, and I don't care how beautiful or how ugly you are, if that has been your ticket you are a loser — a loser.

The great school of ancient wisdom is not about ancient

bodies. It is the development of the invisible, the substantive aspect. You get there by understanding the modus operandi, the ulterior motive. When you have built spiritual substance in yourself is when you love who you are. That is transcendent of the body. Those are the lofty ones that get to go on because what they really are is that substance, and they can detach from the body and have no other dealings with it. Easy, why? Because most of the days of their life they are out of their body, meaning not that they have vacated it but their thought process isn't spent solely on it, and during their everyday life they are thinking in terms of different realms. Their passion has not to do with the body. It has to do with life. It has to do with God and its manifestation. To come down from that lofty high and have to fix the body is a downer for these people. It is a downer to them.

This is not an ancient school about bodies but it is a school that trains the great self to be dominant over them. It is that great self that ultimately is going to be reviewing this life — this life, this body, a garment in the closet of lifetimes. And what was the fruitful experience? Remember why we are here. We are here to make known the unknown, not to hold onto the known but to be the unknown, not to be the known but to be the unknown. That is why we are here. That is why the Spirit starves in the cadaver. That is the reason why the personality can't get a clue of what it is, and it suffers so much because it is so based upon flesh and blood and bones and the way genetics threw you together.

Now I know that this is philosophical, premium stuff. But the fact of the matter is, it isn't practical in day-to-day life unless one has a passion to understand its truth enough to be able to live it. Therein those who do this get the keys to the kingdom of heaven because it is something that must be lived. You are not the sum total of the mass from which you are made. You are not it. And for you to sit out here and say, "Well, this is just the way that I am," fine. When you get tired of being just the way you are, come see me. We can fix it. We can change, because the nature of us is the divine.

Now there are so many variables that work into this life review. There is not a person in this audience that isn't going to be brought to their knees when you see it, because there is nothing in your life that you have done that is without shame. You have done many things with shame and most of it when you knew better. That is when the true shame comes and that is when the working — the working — of that conscious action starts to fix the personality and fixes the hardwiring up in the brain. You are then going to find it is a very difficult hole to crawl out of, but it is about rewiring. It is about today you are learning knowledge, which knowledge will become apparent in your life when you have infused it into your neuronet and start to make that knowledge the goal of your thinking process every day. Then you will see the results of this knowledge. Now you are starting to see the action of the divine starting to take place in your life — fruitful change, miraculous.

There is no one in this audience who cannot change — no one. Now what things do you change? Think about if you were to review your life right now. What if today you got to spin out those bands and see everything from every point of view — from the Godhead, from the spiritual point of view, from the soul, personality — what would you change today? If you know the answer to that, then you don't have to die today and be reborn ignorant again. If you know the answer to what is it that you would change in yourself when you are everything, everyone, and all the environment in your life, what ulterior motive are you going to change? If you know the answer to that today, you will never have to die in this life. People die because they don't know the motive of their existence. That is it. When you look at that on the other side, it becomes so apparent.

This is where the training of being the Observer is so marvelous, because the Observer becomes detached from the personality and the emotional body. It can observe from every angle one's intention — intention — the arrow, where it goes. It can observe it and see it and be it at all places. To be detached and be the Observer is difficult because you are most afraid of your own criticism — you yourself. It is you who are afraid of your Observer. You can deceive other people but you can't deceive yourself. You are afraid to switch modes, because the moment you do you are going to see what you have really been, and it is from that point of view that the light has its most profound effect. Know yourself and you will be free. When you can become the Observer and observe your actions this life and find out your modus operandi, your ulterior motive, it also means that the personality will become criticized. It becomes threatened, and it will. As the Observer you can freely admit it. The moment you switch back and become the personality, you are going to suffer emotion from it. You are going to cry and weep and deny — that is all your imagination — but these are the qualities that do the review and indeed these are the qualities that allow you to go on to the Plane of Bliss.

You don't have to die to do that. You can do it here. What is then the process of that? Long contemplation and being acutely aware of how you are with different people. What is your agenda? How are you with nature? What is your agenda? How are you in your work? What is your agenda? How are you in your family? What is your agenda? What is it? How are you in your sexual life? What is the agenda there, the real agenda? Look at it. Don't be afraid to look at it, and when you do and you can find it, I tell you, beautiful people, it will become real clear. It is simple;

it is not complex. You don't need a psychiatrist to figure this one out, and they never do figure anything out. You just need to know for yourself, and it will all be individual. The moment you know that, the one thing you must dissolve in the crucible is that motive. That is what goes into the crucible and must be dissolved. That is the place you change, right there, because to change on the surface is not to change its nucleus.

You can change on the surface. You can switch partners, like so many of you do, go through each other like flies. You can switch partners. You can move, move around a lot. You can get rid of things, get new things. You can go out and throw away the old clothes, buy new clothes, throw away the new clothes, get old clothes. It doesn't matter. It is all just the surface but that doesn't affect the nucleus. The nucleus of you, and your job here, is the ulterior motive. That is what must be changed. When it is changed, it in turn will affect profoundly the entire environment around you. That is when the dross of your life starts to drop, and here is the true test. God doesn't test you, and everyone here uses the words, "Well, it is a test." Well, there is no test. There is no one keeping score somewhere. It is simply choice, and if you call choice a test, then so be it. But, you see, there are no tests; there are just choice and opportunity. The moment everything starts to fall apart because you have disrupted the nucleus and changed it, if you start suffering from the outward effects of that nuclei change in the self, the temptation is to paste it and put it back together because you can't emotionally handle, personalitywise, what you have done in a loftier venue, the Observer. You can't handle emotion because the Observer is not emotional, and you are not going to know what you have done until you have moved back into the personality. Then all hell breaks loose and you see it all.

Now everyone says, "Well, it was a real test. What am I

going to do with this now? Am I going to run back? Well, I can't bear it. I feel such guilt, and I don't want that person to have this person. I can't fathom him sleeping with this person. I can't fathom it. I can't tolerate it. I can't this, I can't that. I can't lose my children. I can't lose my home. I can't lose my point of view. I can't. I can't. I can't. I can't." And, you see, what has started in a nuclear reaction coming from Point Zero into a biophysical reaction is can you carry it all the way through and let it fall apart? Can you do that without pasting it and putting it back together? It isn't a test.

Here is the warning that I always tell you: Don't go back to your past. That is exactly what I mean by that. Once you have changed, don't go change the change. Don't go glue it back together. The temptation — because you are emotional, personality creatures — is to do exactly that and draw the line in the sand, territorially speaking. What happens then? You go back to your past through emotion. What is emotion? Guilt, shame, fear, insecurity, envy, threat, power. Those are all the emotions that cause the swing all the way back. If you hold that emotion and go back and paste it together, then you are going to have a problem because the nucleus change that has occurred is not reflecting the physical one that has now been put back into place, and now we have great contention.

Some of you might know that when you went back to your past and did paste it up, it was never the same. Why wasn't it the same? Because something fundamentally had changed. Even though you went back and put it back together, there was a change that happened. What happens in those situations? All emotions become heightened — heightened. Why? Because the ulterior motive has changed, that is why. An emotion has to stand on its own. It doesn't have the fundamental support of the ulterior motive any longer, so emotion is hysterical.

All of this understanding is a prelude now to an action graphic that you are going to draw a little bit later to understand what is intent coming into reincarnation. You are going to understand that.

Being an Honorable and Impeccable Person

I want to pause here for a moment and mention what honor is. Everyone — everyone — cherishes that word honor, to be honorable. Everyone wants to be somehow honorable. It seems to be a noble and befitting way to be, but I will tell you what honor is. Honor is when you don't play games and simply are your ulterior motive. That is being impeccable. That is not necessarily beautiful but that is impeccable. That is being honorable. That is being up-front and the way that it is. There is no mishmash. There is no gray area. There is no maybe. There is no hot and cold: one day you are on, the next day you are off. There is no instability. When you are what you are at this time in your time, as it is known, that is being honorable and indeed impeccable. To waver off of that is to be unimpeccable. Do you not then find truth in the axiom that there is honor among thieves? Isn't there? Yes. And cannot then your enemy — the enemy, your most awesome enemy — be closer to you than your lover? Absolutely.

This is what I call an impeccable person. That impeccable person I will jolly well enjoy their presence, and I am very picky about who gets into my presence because you always have to deal with the soap opera with people who have ulterior motives and you are always having to deal with them. Like a soap bubble, they are changing colors and they are filmy and never want to really know. You always have to entertain them or not talk to them at all because they are not impeccable people. They are not who they are. They are pretenders. They are an imitation. They are not genuine. There are a lot of disingenuous people sitting in this audience hearing this message. You are disingenuous because you don't live in your life what you have learned here. You are disingenuous because you take what you have learned here and use it as a pretense while all along coveting a rotten nature, covering your ulterior motive. That is why you are not consistent in this school.

Now you can be consistent as a scoundrel out there. Scoundrels find their cards in the discipline of Fieldwork® all the time and lofty people don't find their cards all the time, and vice versa. You understand? It is the ulterior motive. Where are you with this? These soapy, soap-opera people are never genuine. Genuine beings I enjoy, I engage, because with them we have a true interaction, for they have nothing to hide and so when we engage, they engage from a truthful place. When they learn, they learn truthfully — not soapy learning — real learning.

This is no different than at the light, because at the light then everything is uncovered and the soap opera is shown right in front of you, and you are all players and you see how disgusting that is. The one thing that you walk away from it feeling, as the personality aspect of the great self, is that you dishonored yourself — flat-out dishonored — and as a result manipulated other people because of that. You were insincere and unfruitful. I used to call lies creative truths, and they still are creative truths. Creative truth is the avoidance of the motive. When you are what you are, you never, ever have to protect what you say and you never have to worry about what you say because all of your thoughts are written — written — in the energy around you just as if they were written in the sky above.

You never have to worry a hundred thousand years from now those thoughts come back to you, that ulterior motive comes back to you. You will feel no shame for it because the motive was not disingenuous. It was a motive evolving. It did not make a lot of people succumb to it. It wasn't abusive. It was genuine. That is true evolution.

If you dig up fossil remains of present-day animals, you will see that there is a modulation, a change, in who they were ten million years ago versus who they are today. If you look at those remains, you do not say, "Oh, that is bad. That was a mistake. We are much better off today with this one." You do not see evolution in those terms. You simply see the fossil from where it was in its past to where it is today. You see through geological age the evolution of that species, and you celebrate that it changed. It gives you hope for yourself. You never look at what it was and condemn it. You only do that if you are disingenuous.

When you look in the light, if you are honorable people you are going to see your honor. You are going to see that you lived forthrightly what you were and had clear boundaries about it. It is going to become obvious who you were and how it affected everyone. Most certainly it took unique people to live in your life as an honorable person but by the same token you, to them, were the spark of honor in their life. What are you going to view as God when you look at the consequences of every action in the light? Think about this. In the light review you are going to become the person who you mirrored to them that honor, and in that moment you are going to feel their honor. It may not be the epic point of evolution but it is the point of evolution of that life. It solidified. It was real. In honor, those that are around you can only be with you because you are that way. They can only love you because they love in you what they love in themselves, that poignant truth, that honor, that nobleness. And it may be backward but it is real. It is tangible. It is substantive. It is not illusionary.

Illusions: When you love an illusion, it says that you are only one yourself. That is why it never lasts. Relationships based upon illusionary love are an illusion and both participants are illusionary. They never last. It is like the vapor when the sun hits it, it dissipates. When real heat comes into the relationship, it dissipates because it is an illusion. It is ulterior motive to ulterior motive and soap in between, a nice lubricant.

Could It Be That You Are Already Dead?

This I am telling you now you have seen before — many times before or you wouldn't be here — and you are going to see it again. And when you see this in the life review — when you see today that this is the grand, grand booby prize of this school — you get to live over again, after you die, every class you ever attended. A little extra on the side for when you cross over. You see, right now — listen to me, can you think this way? — right now you are viewing what you are doing right now from the other side. You are viewing it. It is already happening. You are the entity being viewed. Think about this. Don't get linear with me. Think about this. Right now you are dead and on the other side, and you are viewing this life. It is happening right now — right now.

What are you hearing on the other side? Yes, what are you hearing? What am I telling you? What are you thinking? Well, you are seeing it right now. It is unfolded. It is in your time-flow. What am I telling you? What are you hearing? It is happening right now. You are watching this and you are already gone. All you are is remembering this participation. Could that be? Could it be? Now wait a minute. Is this the only reality you are living in or are you a multiple-reality being? If you are, you are already there and you are living what you are viewing right now. Remember, in God you are eternal. You are the past, present, and future simultaneously. When you are a human being, you are only the past struggling for a future, but in God it has already happened.

Are you thinking? Are you visualizing without time? Can you do that? If you can do that, you are what great masters are made of because they also possess the ability to disenfranchise time. That means to actually remove time as the dominant factor.

Let's go over this again. Could it be that you are already dead? Yes? It is true. Am I speaking to an audience of the underworld? Why not? Why can't you entertain that? Because if you can entertain that, then you are very loosely tied to your body. If you can't, you are going to have problems. Why can't you entertain that maybe you are really already dead and this class is being held right now in the light review and this is one of the classes that you are attending. Keep scratching. You are going to get it. Why not? What kind of Master Teacher would I be if I told you that it wasn't so? This is how a Master God thinks. Don't you understand I have just given you a dynamic secret — a dynamic secret — and that I have just made you a dimensional mind. I have just made you for a moment become a dimensional mind and all along you may think that you are really alive. Maybe you are just dead, reliving a moment in the light. Don't you give me that business, "Oh, that is not real." It is more real than you think this place is.

You are in school today. Why are you here? You are learning about the very thing that you are watching right now. You are learning about it and you want to know, "How do I flip this? What do I do with this teaching? Where do I put this?" It is wonderful; you have no place to put it. You have no place to put it. That is even more beautiful. If you put it over into your imagination, then it doesn't serve you. If you put it over here and just say it is a potential trick question, it will serve you but, you see, both have not been integrated. Here is the idea: You are already dead. You are in the light and you are viewing this and you have come back and you are reliving this experience. Why? To understand the key of being red in the rainbow, to understand why you have to do this again, and when you find the key, what can you do with that. If you find the key, you have flipped back into this life from being dead. You have flipped back into this life and you have a new agenda. You have been reincarnated in an immortal body. We are going to talk about immortality in context of the living, vital energy called an idea.

I want to remind you that between life and death there is no distinction in the Spirit. There is none. There is no life or death in the Spirit. There is only life and death to the individual personality and its cohabitating body, but to the Spirit and the Godhead, there are no clear distinctions between the two. I want to remind you that what I have told you could be happening right now — and it is. So why are you here? To learn something, a key, understanding something, to understand a key, a bit of knowledge, to know what to ask, to know what to suddenly turn on and to know, because this is what the Plane of Bliss is all about.

There is a real reason why true masters gain the stewardship over the physical. They die to the physical, first off. Somewhere in their initiation they die to the physical. What that means is that they are no longer concerned with the physical. They die to the world. They are reborn into the life of an initiate, a master, where there are no clear lines of life and death. They can flip right into such a scene like this and review it and relive it over and over and over without ever having to die in the body. Who is to say that of all the potentials that exist, do you know that you cannot exhaust the ideas, the things that can be manufactured from atoms? You cannot even exhaust the probability of potentials that they can become, and all they are is coagulated ideas in the form of energy. You cannot exhaust it. You cannot think long enough in a lifetime to make them become everything that they have the potential of becoming. Who is to say that you have not already flipped back into this time? Who is to say that you are one of those masters on the other side that is this close — this close? You have flipped back into this time. You have died to this life review. You are reviewing it — you are reviewing it — something you have missed. You have the power to do that.

Why would you want to do that without going through the ability just to die? Why not give up this physical body? I mean, it is certainly a trap. It is a prison. I don't care how you look at it, it is a prison. Why not just give it up? You have the power to leave your body. Get out of here. Why then do real masters learn the art of longevity and immortality? Why? There must be a reason that they want to preserve this, and it isn't about their looks and it isn't about how many orgasms they can have and it isn't about how much food they can eat. They want to preserve it. It is not about how curvaceous the body is. It has nothing to do with appearance. They died to that a long time ago because when they were born spiritual, they could love nothing but the spiritual.

Now why would they want to preserve this body? Why are they here? I can tell you that only a few of you — some of you, not all of you — are real masters flipping back into this death scene. You are on the other side and you are living this. Why are you doing that? Because there is something you are going to know about yourself that you are going to have a passionate fire about, and when you unlock ulterior motives you will have unlocked the power of the nucleus. You have absolute radiant, atomic energy. That is what is locked inside ulterior motive. Why then would you want to flip back into this scene that you are dead viewing this in an incarnation? What would be the reason? Because if you can gain in this school in the light of something that you are revisiting over and over, you are going to pull out of it the question that only you have the answer to that is going to unlock immortality in the body on the other side of this light review, and you want that.

Why do you want that? Because in order to make known the unknown, the immortality of the body is as much a mystery and a desire as any desirous, seductive food or entertainment to the lifetime of the body. You want to master the longevity of the physical, and only a powerful Spirit can do that. Only an enlightened being can do that. Only an entity with fortitude, will, and intent can do that. Why? Because that is the true manifestation of the image of God, and it is through such beings that the great and marvelous deeds of God are revealed.

All masters are immortals. Does it mean that they are caught forever in this body? Just however they want it. They have it on their own terms. They can flip that body into its rainbow body, into its golden body, into its Blue Body, all the way back to its flesh body, its lightbody, its infrared body. They are lord of the entire ladder, of all dimensions. They never have to die. They have conquered it. And what comes with such a powerful, spiritual intent? The seeds of immortality itself. You cannot have an ulterior motive of immortality from a spiritual intent and not have the substance of it in your life.

There are some of you that have gone backwards in time and are dead, reviewing this moment that happened a long time ago right now, working to understand what was not understood before, knowing it is an opportunity. In this moment, if in the light you are a participant as Observer and God, then that master brings back to this the entire self on all levels, and that self has no problems seeing this conjunction of time happening right here. They have no problem seeing it. A truly physical person will have a lot of problems understanding this, not a spiritual person because to them manifestation has nothing to do with its coagulation in time but has everything to do with its coagulation in thought. That is a spiritual person. A material person is just the opposite.

I already know who is going to come out of this school. I already know my place with them. I already know. That is a certitude. Does revisiting this then afford what wouldn't have come out as the opportunity to bloom from it? Yes. Why do we know that? Because if that were not true, there would be no law of incarnation. There would not be reincarnation. There would not be the transmigration of the Spirit and the soul, and yet there is. Why? Cannot time double up on itself? Of course it can. And what, I tell you, bends time? Mind, that is what bends time. Mind is the subject of God, and only between the two does time exist.

When you revisit the light in this life, are you given another opportunity to polish, to improve, to pick up what you didn't hear the first time, what you didn't feel the first time? If you revisit the same situation with improved knowledge, is the scene going to change? Always. That is the law of making known the unknown. How many times do you have to go back to the light and review the same source material from the soul until you change it? You understand that knowledge and its integration into mind is the fire that changes it. When you revisit your weakest point with knowledge is when you change it.

How many times have you heard this message from me? Does anyone dare to guess? How many times have you revisited this session in the light? How many times has this teaching happened? This day, the way you look, the way your neighbor looks, how many times have you seen this? Don't you get a feeling of déjà vu a little bit? Is this the only time today ever happened? You think this is it, this event came and went? How many times have I stood up here and given this teaching? How many times have I taught beginners? How many times have I taught about Point Zero and the great vast nothingness — how many times — in your short career in coming to this school? Well, I have done today more than those times. I keep saying the same thing. I vary it. Why do I vary it? Because you have been varied. You are ready to hear, ready to see, ready to feel. You are not, you are dead. You are dead.

I want you to draw a picture, put it down in an abstract graphic seeing this in the light, and that you are already dead and that you are about to be reborn, and you thought you were alive all along. You draw that. Draw it and color it. Why do I want you to do that? Because I want this knowledge to be in your brain. At the end of the day you are supposed to know something that the soul knows, and unless you can draw it and color it, you are not going to know it and you are going to have to revisit this day again. So be it.

Do We Choose Our Parents in Our Next Reincarnation?

God bless,
embrace,
and allow
all the voices
of my total self
to be heard
and be seen.
So be it.
To life.

I want you to make this drawing and explain it as the Observer. You need to have your perspective blown in order to understand the last teaching I gave you. I endeavor to keep this very simple so that you can grasp what it is that you are here to understand again.

Remember what you first learn when you come to my school about Point Zero, primary consciousness.[8] Just color in a black dot and over to the side write primary consciousness. The purple dot is secondary consciousness. Notice that I have a green extension there. The green dot is the soul, and the soul rides along with secondary consciousness. It is the recorder of events. The red dot, or circle, is the incarnation, the body itself, body/mind consciousness — body/mind consciousness. In other words, we have to credit the body with having its own intelligence, which it does. It is a conscious intelligence, a biophysical, sentient being.

---

8 See Ramtha, *A Beginner's Guide to Creating Reality*. Third edition (Yelm: JZK Publishing, a division of JZK, Inc., 2004).

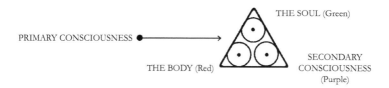

Now this is the order in which they come. The great self is constituted by the integration of these four elements we drew. Whether this body is a sixth-plane body, a fifth-plane body, a fourth-plane body, a third-plane body, a second-plane body, or a first-plane body, it is a body. This body then is held together by that which is termed the spiritual body of secondary consciousness, and what holds them all together is called the Holy Spirit, which is the spiritual interaction of the complete self. This is where we get the idea of a triad. Let's go back to the beginning teachings to understand better your incarnation from the Plane of Bliss or perhaps your present revisiting to this school.

I want to ask you a very important question: Why would you not believe my last statement that you are already dead and you are in a light review right now? Why wouldn't you believe that? Why isn't it believable? It is a very powerful question because it has everything to do with the intrinsic knowledge that you have incorporated about time and space and consciousness. It tells you the degree of that knowledge that you bear. This body/mind consciousness would never believe what I have just told you. It would see it as a fanciful imagination, a paradigm — a monad, if you will — but they would never believe it because they can point to their body and say, "Look, I can pinch this body and it hurts. Look, I don't know what that person is thinking. Look, I visited the graveyard and I am not buried anywhere — yet."

I want to tell you something. If this becomes the choice factor by which you determine reality, then you will wholly disbelieve the potentials in which you can exist. In other words, you have sided with your body. You really have. You have sided with the body because you cannot quite believe that this is possible. Well, what does that tell you? That tells you that if you side with the body, the joke is on you because you continue to live and you say, "See there, I am continuing to live. One day I am going to die." Is it possible that in doing that, you are living in a delusionary illusion? Absolutely.

Why would you want to side with your body? What is the upside to this? What if you sided with these two, primary and secondary consciousness? Why secondary consciousness? Because it is the Spirit in the body. It contains the spiritual body in which the soul itself rests. And, remember, the soul keeps track of who you have been. It catalogs what you are, so it is the carrier, if you will, of the memory of personality. If you have looked at a cadaver recently, you wonder where the person is. You look at the mouth you kissed, the eyes that used to dance, the animation in the hands, the softness of the touch, or the athleticism of movement of the body, and you look at it and it is stiff and hard and lifeless. It is lifeless. It is. What left it? Secondary consciousness, the soul personality, is what left it. Is that really you? That is really a part of you.

Now if you could accept today this teaching that you really are in a light review right now — and that you are actually reviewing who you are in a classroom that has to do with exactly the subject matter in which you are involved, ironically — if you could believe that and have room to accept that, that speaks of a great graduation of evolution of your own personal consciousness. It means that you are so lofty that the idea that you are actually in a light review is not astonishing at all.

Why would that be to your advantage to side with primary and secondary consciousness on this issue? Obviously because those are the selves that remain when birth and death go on as cyclical reincarnation. They remain. What other advantage is there? Here is the advantage. If you really believe what I told you today — you really believed it — by the end of this day you would know your ulterior motive. And because you will know it, you will change it. What sort of dynamics are going to spin off of that change? What are they going to be? It must be as real to you as the denial of its reality is to you. It must have that same equal thrust. It must be as real as denial is real, and if it is, then think of the possibilities of what we are looking at here. You are actually in a moment of observable participation in which you have been here before and you are back and so much of this sounds familiar and it starts to come to the surface of your mind. When you reach back to try to look at it, it disappears like vapor, and there is a familiarity to this.

Why is it important to believe that it is possible? Because in the cyclical reincarnation — the linear process of birth and death, afterlife, new sojourns — the whole process is to be able to see a life from the vantage point of the all, not just the singular, which is so indigenous to human beings. They are very singular and very separated. They cannot see through the mind of God, only through the mind of the body's personality. It is very self-evident in the way you live. If that were so then, in a light review you would get to see all and you would get to see where your problem is. In that light review you would be able to take and learn a lot about that problem and then meet people on the Plane of Bliss who share the same problem or who share a splintering of that problem. Maybe in one little area that is of no importance to you, but is still a splinter, is a logjam to someone else, and you meet on the Plane of Bliss because you gravitate towards each other. In gravitating towards each other, you work out a relationship that exists there before it exists here, a relationship to which you want this person to come into your life here, and you want the memory and the bonding of it to be so strong on the Plane of Bliss that there is no denying the recognition. There seems to be an instant acceptance of that individual — a harmony, if you will, even a disharmony — because all of those factors, if you have done it correctly, then are incarnated into a life to which as blind men and women you struggle to uncover the mystery, the great unfathomable mystery, of what you are doing here. What is this person trying to tell me about myself and what indeed am I trying to tell me about myself, because they are reflections of what I am. That is all they are. They are here to teach you lessons, or maybe you are both here to gain a lesson to various degrees. Why do you need that lesson? Well, because it is daunting. This subject matter keeps reappearing, and so everyone becomes a player in everyone's life.

Now the only difficult thing is — and I always said this, and here I part ways with New Age thinking to some degree because they don't have all the information — it was always broadly understood that you choose your parents. In the naiveness of the human culture, they simply think that you go to that big parent garden in the sky and you say, "I will take you and you," and that they know beforehand who those parents are going to be. That is not correct. It has truth in it but it is not solid, substantial truth.

The way it works is that whatever your issues are, whatever you have decided on Bliss that is the next level that you have to work on — which is really the same thing you worked on two thousand years ago, and through successive generations and technological changes you have made little progress — you are still in a problem. The whole world is. You are still dealing with this issue that is two thousand years old. This is not something of the twentieth century, technological-based, rapid-growing, artificial-life century. This is an issue that goes way back, and what is so frustrating about it is that it is a very simple thing. But what is simple to the Spirit is so difficult for the human because the human becomes complex by its emotions.

What happens is that you have formulated what you come to learn here on the plane of demonstration. You don't pick your parents. You are drawn to a genetic pool that is no greater than the question you asked. Why should that not have continuity to it? God only knows what you know. Why should you be drawn to a genetic pool that knows more than you? You are not going to be. You will only manifest in reality — whether it is atomic structures, cellular biology, whether it is environmental, thought, ideas — what you are equal to and what accommodates the learning here. You do pick your parents on an issue of like-begging-like, but as far as descriptiveness, you don't. Now there are people who have an issue with bodies and have always had an issue with bodies. They always vacillate to those who can produce to them the best bodies, but that is body/mind consciousness, and that is self-evident too because the greatest asset is that and nothing else.

What about geniuses? My God, don't you know the most brilliant minds that ever came were from very simple stock. That was amazing, wasn't it? It was almost as if the genetic stock itself was not complex but simple. In other words, the genes had clear windshields so that what you brought through to it could clearly be brought forward into a life, a mind could grow and flourish. You can grow and flourish as exquisite flowers in a simple garden. If it is cluttered, you get choked out by weeds and other shrubbery and the like.

Then you are born — and I want all of you to think about your body — exactly with the genetic body that is the utility to match and work through your altered agenda, your karma, your lesson, finishing it. This is quite amazing because then you begin to look at bodies and it becomes really clear who chose what and for what reason. Everything is a story. Ulterior motives can be seen in the body, literally can be seen in the body. You are born into a family. Who are these families? Does it mean that your brothers and sisters with whom you share an incarnation came from the same place on the Plane of Bliss? No, because the genetic pool which they came through offered primitive or advanced opportunities. They are different levels, but the body suits them.

Now I want to ask you this question again: Why would you disbelieve that you are in a light review? Why would you want to do that? I will tell you. Victims want to do that and materialistic people want to do that and carnal people want to do that. When they can deny this possibility that I have given to you earlier — when they can deny this — then they have no threat to change their life, no excuse. They say, "I am what I am and I can't change. I like what I am. I like to hate what I am and so I don't have to bother." That is very secure ground, isn't it? It is secure. Tomorrow morning you are going to wake up, you will still be in school, but the day after you are going to wake up and you are going to be someplace else. You can count on that. In a body-physical life, you can count on every day waking up and every night going to sleep and in between having fun. That is a sense of security. You have pragmatic minds that will disavow primary consciousness and say that doesn't exist. You will never die? What a fool. Who do you think you are? Go to the graveyard and take a look. There is a little problem with that, you know. Science is starting to wake up with the quantum theory of all potentiality existing simultaneously — all potentiality — and remember what I told you about cosmic atoms. What that means is that you cannot exhaust the potentials utilizing atoms as building blocks.

Now here is something else I want to ask you, a very important question. If you did accept and believed this, how would your life change today if suddenly you said, "Oh, my God, I am in a light review? I am dead? I am actually viewing as the Observer how I lived it? And thank God I came to this school because I wouldn't be awake to acknowledge that I should be thinking about this in the light. I am calling out to you from beyond the grave." What are you thinking watching this? What should you be thinking? "My God, this very moment I can change my life because all I am expecting is to see what I remembered that I was."

You know how hard it is to remember the rest of your life? Not very hard. Think about it. If you didn't work in lofty thoughts, how hard would it be to remember the rest of your life? It is pretty predictable, isn't it? You look forward to those nights that you go out and do this and that, and then you go to work, and then you do that, and you have little problems with your family, little squabbles here and there, but you know they are going to be resolved sooner or later. You have a little problem here but it will be all right there. You are then a year older and you are this and you are that. How could you not remember what is yet to come? It has already happened because it is predictable. That predictability is powerful security, and there are people who will deny the opportunity to change for the sake of predictable security. It happens every day.

Now why not believe this? What would happen if that great big, beautiful Orb sitting on top of those shoulders finally clicked and said, "What if I am dead? Here is my chance. What will I do different in my life? What do I come away with from this? What is it that I want more than anything? If I get a chance to live again, what do I want? Oh, my God, I never want to forget this moment. I don't want to be born ignorant. Somehow I want to maintain this moment. I don't want it to be elusive and fly away. I don't want to lose it in the birth canal and I don't want to lose it in youth and I don't want to lose it in reckless adulthood. How do I remember this?"

Think about that. "This moment can change my life. Nothing is set. It is a light review and I am in the midst of it. How do I want to see me right now?" Shine, my beloved people. How do you want to see you? You want to see you as primary consciousness sees you. That is what you want. You don't want to see you as body/mind consciousness sees you, because if you do you are a dead ringer to come back again. Everything is up for grabs. The whole life is over with. "I just thought I was going to an event." Marvelous thought, isn't it? Is it real? Only you know that answer, but if it is real, it is absolute freedom. My God, what do you do with a treasure? How do you want to be from this moment on? "How do I want to see me? How do I want to see me? What is the great reflection that I must shine back to my eventual observation in the light?"

Now think about this. You are going to die. Those of you who are body/mind consciousness, you are going to die. You are going to go to the light because you know about it. You are going to see this day again. Why would your soul leave this day out? Why would it leave this morning out? Is it going to remember all those things you did behind closed doors and forget about this one? No. It has recorded everything. Just like those of you who are taking notes, you are writing the same words your soul is writing but your soul is doing asterisks down here, footnotes, soul notes there at the bottom. Soul notes are the Observer observing the notes being written.

186

Now if this day is going to come again — and you are standing there with your Holy Spirit and your God and it starts to come on — and you have been the great self in every view of this lifetime since the womb on, why would this day be left out? How important is today? Very important. Why? Because what do you want to tell yourself today? What do you want to tell yourself? It is going to be replayed. What do you want to see and hear? What do you want?

I want you to take your paper, your pencil, your writing instrument. Now this is no joke. What do you want to be remembered today that has already happened and is being reviewed now about yourself? Come on, what do you want to hear and see? Anything goes. You would be very wise if you included in this what you have found your ulterior motive to be and be able to say it. Write it down. What is it and how has it served you? It is important that you remind yourself what it is, what you have been, what is the hook that keeps bringing you back here. It is important that you say it.

Having said that, then you must also add to it, being utterly impeccable, whether you are willing to give it up. If you are not — no matter what you see, no matter how many people are hurt, no matter how many people are used and abused, no matter what you have done and how clever you are — if you cannot give it up, you are doomed to relive it again. You are doomed to relive it. You have to cry out to that which is viewing this now what one must change and what one desires to be, and then the great pronouncement, the great question, the great desire, must follow.

What does this have to do with the Plane of Bliss? Everything.

Near-Death Experiences and the Egyptian Rites of Passage

It is reported that entities who have near-death experiences, when they fully have one, that the experience enriches them and changes them marvelously and they are never who they used to be. Who they used to be will never be recaptured again. Why? Because in a single life they had a heart attack, they drowned, they were electrocuted, they took a fatal dose of something, and they got out of their body and went so far as the great life review. Some of them went all the way through a life review and they got to see the self from all perspectives. They got to be the self from all perspectives except that aspect called God, that great being that poured out unconditional and profound love. They all say that they were connected to this being, and yet this was God. They weren't advanced enough to know that the great, radiating being was them as God. They didn't know that but they suspected an interconnectedness with everything. They got to look at to whom they were married, their children, their problems, their issues of success and failure, their prejudices, their ulterior motives.

How great is the ulterior motive of someone who wants to kill themselves? People who kill themselves do it out of revenge for other people. That is the way they get back — it is — make someone else sorry. What is the ultimate trip you can lay on someone? That is the ultimate trip. Now that is an exaggeration, but a heart attack is the failure of living. It is the failure of expression. It is holding things together that should be let go. It is, in its way, a suicide.

They get there and suddenly see all of those things, and they see the impact that they have created in other people's lives. They see that and suddenly become so understanding of the importance of life. In other words, they wake up in the light review. They wake up in the light review and that is why they get to come back. That is why they get to come back and resurrect that dead body lying on that table, that machine starting up that heart again or those chemicals being thrust into the body to cause brain-wave activity to occur. They get to come back to that body. What a deliverance. And when they come back and they awaken, they are not the same people who only moments earlier lived in that same body. They are different, profoundly different. Their views on life are so drastically altered to make one suspect that this cannot be the same person. Why am I telling you this? Because all that they get to experience, you get to experience today and tonight in the same manifesto. You have to know this day is inevitable. Know it, because it is.

Why is it so important? Because maybe it has already happened. Maybe this is the opportunity to see in a review what has doggedly plagued you all of your life. Perhaps it is the day that you wake up and realize the value of what you get to have on the other side of this day. What is the difference? Maybe you are already dead. Do you think I will wait and worry about that when I die? Maybe you already are and the joke is on you because, you see, you should live every day consciously and not postpone it. Every day should be primary — not secondary or body/mind consciousness — primary, because that is what fires the Spirit of secondary every day. Why do you think this is something that you can wait and play around with? How do you know how beautiful your life is about to be? How do you know? What did you just say to be remembered? You are going to be saying it tonight. You are going to be talking to yourself tonight and it will be remembered and will be played back. What are you going to want to hear?

What is going to make the difference? When you are doing a light review, you are going to tell your body — you are going to tell your life — "Look, I am your memory. I was in anticipation of now. Let me tell you what I want. I have been dead. I have been uninspired. I have lived as a human being struggling for the rapture of spiritual countenance. I have desired it but I haven't done it yet — yet. Remember me. I am telling you this. What do I want? I want this day in my life to be remembered as the day I fell apart and was reborn to a change — a fundamental, ingrained change in me. I want you to remember that because whether it is today or the day after, this day has already happened and surely will come."

What do you want to say? "Wait, you have time. You, I want you to resurrect my body. I want you to go back, but I want you to go back with this knowledge. I do not want to be born again in another body. I get to say my piece. Listen to me. I want another chance, but I don't want to forget. I want to know and remember. Thus you go back to the body and you revive it and put me in there consciously altered and changed. What do I want to be altered? I don't want to be a limited human being again. I don't want the value of myself being based upon my body. I want the value of myself being based upon the consciousness of what flowers from within me. I do not want to play games anymore. I want the reality of the manifesto of the great arcanum. I want to be a living fire master. You go back to that body and you wake up."

No one told you to say that. I am telling you to say that because you have already died. I am telling you that you must be immortal in an incarnation. You don't need to incarnate. You only need to wake up now.

You say, "What is the problem? I am not getting this now." You know what the problem is? It is because you haven't realized what has held you back, where your power is coagulated. It is coagulated in your ulterior motives. That is where your real passion is. Passion is power, and if you are trying to start something new and it isn't in alignment with your ulterior motive, you are not going to have the passion to bring it to fruition. This has to be your passion. If you were as passionate about today as you are about your ulterior motive, you will live forever consciously — forever. You will live forever. How do I know that? Because I am that. This primary consciousness and this entity here must agree. The agreeance is the Holy Spirit and the power of the Holy Spirit. These are who you are. They are going to live anyway. But what about them? Why do we need this? Because we are unfinished with this stage of exploration, and the truth is we cannot be this primary consciousness fully and richly until we have been that in this secondary consciousness, until this mirrors that. When you do, you will only have primary consciousness.

Now who says I dare you that such a command would not be hastened to? Who is going to stop you, God and his angels? You are God and his angels. Who is going to stop you? The only person that is going to stop you is you. You know why you are going to stop you? Because you don't believe that. That is why. But I am telling you, you are going to put the message down because this day is going to be played again and someone has to remind you what do you say in the midst of a life review. What do you say? When do you wake up in the dream and when do you command the dream? What is going to happen when you say to you — you turn right around in the light review and you are looking at you — "I know you are watching me now. I know you are watching me. You, who went on, I am giving you a message now because you are going to see me again. I am you. I am what I look like in the body. You are viewing me outside of that body. Let me tell you what I want you to do. Remember me. If I am buried, so is your wisdom that you have learned. You are not going to pick a genetic child that is going to be fully opened. You remember me. Come back after me and bring this knowledge with you, that I am resurrected into the life that I command you to resurrect me today." What do you think is going to happen? Consciousness and energy creates the nature of reality.

What is initiation? What is resurrection? What is the resurrected death and rebirth? What is that initiation for? It is to prepare you how to act. What is The Egyptian Book of the Dead? The Egyptian Book of the Dead is to teach the sovereign what to do the moment it is out of its body: what to say, where to go, who to see, what to do. They are enchanted with it. Why are the priests saying prayers twenty-four hours a day reciting those passages, reciting them over and over and over? Because that priest is in the light review of that sovereign. That priest is praying for that sovereign, and that sovereign in the light review is hearing the priest from the other side. Don't you understand? Why is it necessary to pray for the souls of the departed? Don't pray unless you have something to tell them.

What if such a command were in the hands of a skillful arbitrator? Aleph, who has one hand in heaven and one foot on the Earth — that is the supreme arbitrator — can reach into heaven and reach into the Earth. That is a master.[9] What if then a master arbitrator knows exactly where to reach and find you on the other side and what they want to say to you? Then the chanting is going to be seen, and they chant over and over and

---

9 Egyptian Goddess Nut. Her appearance is that of a woman whose body arches across the sky, wearing a dress decorated with stars. Nut was the sky Goddess whose body created a vault or canopy over the Earth. Nut was the sister/wife of Geb, the God of the Earth. She was also the mother of Isis, Osiris, Nepthys, and Seth. The ancient Egyptians believed that at the end of the day, Nut swallowed the Sun God Ra and gave birth to him again the next morning. In the light of Ramtha's teachings, the Goddess Nut represents the interim place where the soul rests and reviews its life after death.

over and over, riding Nut all the way over until the weighing of
the heart, the weighing of the soul over and over and over. The
weight must be to a feather over and over and over. How much
is that sovereign going to see that is not going to be featherlike?
A great deal. What is it that it is going to keep seeing though
when it sees the scale? A feather. How is it going to be weighed?
Against a feather. Who is weighing it? Itself[10]

THE EGYPTIAN GODDESS NUT

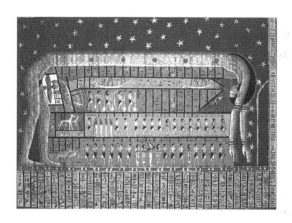

THE PAPYRUS OF ANI — WEIGHING OF THE HEART AGAINST A FEATHER

---

10 See the Papyrus of Ani, popularly known as The Egyptian Book of
the Dead, where the heart of the individual is weighed against a feather in
judgment after death.

This is all happening at the same time, the same moment. So who is going to say the chants for you in your passing? Who did say them? Who is the greatest arbitrator at that vulnerable moment? You are. What are you going to say? "Get back here and be enlightened. For God's sake, dig me up and let's get on with this."

And you say, "I don't want that body any longer. It hurt too much. I am so happy to be free of this cumbersome prison." And you are going to say to it, "I know what you are thinking up there." You are saying this to you in the light. "I know what you are thinking, how good it feels not to have me. You feel so great because you don't have me anymore, because I don't have a headache and I don't have a backache and I am not this and I am not that and I am heavy and I like to eat. And you are thinking you are better off without me. Listen to me. We will be better off together if you come back for me and make me the way you want me. Make me in the image of God." If you do, you will never have to die again and you will never have to be reborn again.

One day when you have the opportunity — one fine morn or one splendid evening — to sit down with a gathering of masters, you will have earned the right to be there because you will have, for a period of time, changed enough to literally think as they think. Today's teaching is how they think.

CHAPTER 7
WHEN YOU LOVE YOURSELF ENOUGH

*"When you love yourself enough to go back, then you
are going to join a great group of masters because you
are going to come back, and that heart is going to
start beating, and you are bringing cognizant memory
here and power. You can then erase age, you can
create glamour, you can become young, old, whatever.
You have the power."*

— *Ramtha*

To a Master There Is No Birth and Death, Only Creation

To a master there is no birth and death. There just isn't.
That is an illusion. There is nothing but the continuity of their
ability to dream states of reality. In order to hold a meaningful
dialogue with a master, you would have to hold it on such levels
of thought like this one because to be anything else, to become
contracted and go back down into the selfish human would not
be a conversation that would be attractive to them. They are not
attracted to soap bubbles, they are not attracted to soap operas,
and they are not attracted to fickle people.

How would that be possible then? For example, today if
this is a light review and you are in the midst of it and you have
been given a powerful orientation — and if this is meaningful
to you and you believe that this actually could be — you have
credited yourself with a quantum leap in evolution. You have
actually set up what has already been and will become, and you
have given yourself instructions and directions of exactly what
you want. Now those are the proper things to be able to do.

How many people go to the light every moment and do not
know this? How many people could not fathom that they are
already dead and they are just reviewing their life? How many
people do you know can fathom that? Not very many. It is not a
conversation that you have in your salon or in the meat market.
It is not just any conversation but a rare conversation, and yet
everything should be done as if it is being done in the light of all
eternity. You cannot prove to me that you are not dead — you
cannot — because then you would have to prove the existence
that you are alive, and how do you do that?

How would you then get to gather with eagles? How would
you get to gather with masters? What brings that into fruition?

196

Now this is the part that we are going to study in depth.

Remember at your beginning event — which is so vastly important to begin in this school, because without this knowledge you are lost — we started with this little Point Zero, which was the child of the Void, one vast nothing materially and all things potentially, and the only way that it can do anything is to create the stage of something. It certainly is not going to have that interaction with the Void because the Void has no parameters in which to fundamentally set up the stage of time. Time is important because it is what allows energy to become a coagulated force in an idea. And isn't it interesting that you had to go within to contemplate to become expanded. That is the greatest law that has set into motion all of life on all planes, in all spectrums, in all planets, in all pasts, in all times to come. It was this simple concept here of contemplation.

What was the reason that we had these two — Point Zero and its mirror, primary and secondary consciousness — that between them was a rarefied atmosphere just like the Earth's atmosphere? From the Earth to the sun there is an atmosphere that is shared between the two. Between primary and secondary consciousness there is an atmosphere which is exactly like the atmosphere you have here. Now this is what is so important that I want you to remember. How do I know you are God and how do you know that for certain? Because you came apart right from the beginning and began contributing to the atmosphere of life. The energy that is being exchanged between primary and secondary consciousness is an energy wave. We can determine what frequency exists on what level by the anatomy of the frequency itself — how short it is or how long it is — and we have a good understanding from where that energy is coming.

For example, superquarks, as it were — transient tachyons that only appear for brief moments in time, which are so brief that you can't even put down here — must come from an extraordinary atmosphere. And what is an extraordinary atmosphere? Remember this: Atmosphere is that which exists between two points of consciousness, and the only two points of consciousness are primary and secondary. A tachyon is a burst, a brief moment in time, but comes from a different time, a different atmosphere, and so it is elusive down here. It is elusive in this atmosphere because it is an alien. It belongs somewhere else. I also taught you that this is actually an enfolding and an unfolding. This is an enfolding and an unfolding from the Void, from primary consciousness to secondary consciousness. And what happens? It is carrying an intent, consciousness, an idea, so that when it collapses it has the intelligence to become something.

"Become something? Wait a minute. I thought this energy was coming out of me."

It is.

"I thought it was bouncing back on the mind of God."

It is. But when it engages from God to you and you both agree, then you give life to the thing. In the beginning, the atmosphere between primary and secondary were the children of primary and secondary — the atmosphere. And of what was the atmosphere made? It was made out of energy and particle potentials. Who puts the idea of riding on the energy? Who is responsible for giving energy the notion to collapse and formulate into a concept? Who does that? You think that just happens? Do you think that there is some big pot in the sky in which this stuff rains out and you are not responsible for, that someone else is responsible for? You think it is the sun's fault that this happens? It is you. It has always been you.

What am I telling you? Who created this Earth? Who created that tree out there and who created the insects? Who created the fishes and who created the worms? Who created the bacteria? Who did all of that? Where did this abundance of natural life with an intelligence — by God, even rocks have intelligence — where does the intelligence come from? There are only two places it could have come from: between the two points of primary and secondary consciousness.

"You mean that a rock has intelligence?"

Yes.

"Well, where did it get the intelligence from?"

It got its intelligence by a primitive form of polarization.

"Well, where did the polarization come from?"

From two points of consciousness.

"What were the two points of consciousness?"

Primary and secondary consciousness.

"Well, what in the world were they doing?"

They were creating.

"And what was it they created?"

Thoughts.

"Well, where are the thoughts?"

They are in the rock. Now all life we are and we have been.

I used to tell this wonderful story in the Dialogue days, a wonderful story about what it was and how we created flowers, how we created animals, insects, and how the symbiotic relationship was only a reflection of the symbiotic relationship we as mighty, divine creators shared. This life was just spewing from us because every time we had a thought, the thought was automatic. We didn't have to think about making a rock; the rock just came out of our head. It was a result of our movement. When we as primary and secondary consciousness pulled apart, we started to coagulate things. What are these things? They are those intelligent thoughts that divinely were given birth to when we went analogical.

Where do you think analogical thoughts go? Do you think we just have a copulation of primary and secondary consciousness and that is it and everyone feels terrific and we separate and are friends forever? Well, what happens to that analogical union? What is the reaction from that analogical union? An atmosphere, and the atmosphere is the coagulation of analogical union.

We created this plane of existence. How did we do that? By doing this process, this analogical union, and every time we did it, something was happening. The atmosphere was getting denser, things started coagulating, thoughts and ideas started to take form. What was a form? We had never seen a form before. We didn't know what form was. This was a reaction from an intention that was natural to us. The phenomenon that occurred became reality. We didn't know that. No one told us that. It was the way time worked in energy, and it is exactly where thoughts and ideas went with time. They only spewed forth in an analogical fountain, and we were that.

I am trying to tell you that as we descended down this ladder of involution, we left these vast continents of beautiful, pristine environments. Just think how pristine they must be, because those were the ages of innocence, the ages of true and pure divinity. Those planes must be indescribable. They are. And where did this place come from? From the indescribable. Every time that we affected energy, every time we got separated in the primary course of involution, we began to affect all planes with our ideas. They became impregnated.

Where did the Earth come from? Where did any of the planets come from? Where did the black holes and white holes come from, those quantum tunnels of unfolding and enfolding potential mass and gas? They came from analogical mind and the intelligence from all of you that are here and all of those that aren't, and all of those that are visible and invisible, all of those that live in other dimensions, on other planets, in other galaxies, in other forms, and in other stratums. It came from all of you. Should we consider ourselves then to be in this descent, into a fall? Because there is a multitude of us, should we consider ourselves a spark or a raging fire? We are a raging fire. Never consider yourself a spark. That just isn't good enough. I would never consider myself a spark. I am a raging fire, and that is what you are. How do I know that? Because you can only inhabit the environment to which you gave analogical intelligence. You cannot inhabit an environment to which you have not contributed. You are always where you are and should be.

It hasn't occurred to you yet — but I am very desirous to blow open your mind because this should be so impactful — that the only reason you are in this Earth incarnation is because it is the only place to which you have contributed. Where else then are you going to go from the Plane of Bliss? Think you are going to go to Venus? Think you are going to go to the twenty-third universe? My great school in the twenty-third universe is producing remarkable beings, and they were in the march with you a long time ago. How is it that they got there and they are not here? Because they believed the story that I left them. They believed the story that I told them, the one hundred and twenty days of communion. In that story I told you where I went, an unfathomable, unbearably beautiful place. And those who could understand, they understood. They contributed to that place because therein was where their longing — their real passion — was. Do you now know where your passion is and why you are here? Because it is the only place to which you have contributed.

Those people went to the twenty-third universe because they dreamed a passionate dream of following me, and they went there. They used to be creatures of this world but they are somewhere else. They also had life reviews. They already know what I just taught you, and true masters emerged not too far after that and women were among them. They got it. They understood. They grasped it. It was there for them to have and they never let go of it. They wrestled with God until they got

God down. They were warriors, so that was all right for them to do that. They were a marching army. They understood siege and they didn't give up, so they grasped hold of the concept and conquered it.

If you only get to where you belong, then take a look at your life now. Just take a moment and look at it. You cannot be victimized any longer by anything in your environment and anyone in your environment. You deserve exactly who you have. You deserve them. You deserve exactly what you have in your life. You don't deserve any more or any less. You have exactly what you are worthy of having and to that which you have contributed. You are only going to get those opportunities in your life because that is all to which you have contributed. And you may not even get them because somewhere you haven't believed them into life, for you have been too busy taking care of physical business over here. You can never go where you don't belong. It will never happen. It is against the law of primary and secondary consciousness creating the nature of reality.

Now the environment that you are in, you created it all. What about the lowly worm? How do you think the worm got intelligence? Intelligence then speaks of a soul. Does a worm have a soul? Yes. How did it get a soul? When you became it. From where does a worm get its intelligence? Yes, it is a remarkable creature that works off instinct, but what have we come to learn about instinct? Instinct was a sensitivity that grew into an instinctual, genetic memory. That then creates a sentient being. The sentient being then has intelligence, and where there is a sign of intelligence, there is a remarkable soul according to that intelligence — small, insignificant, yes, but nonetheless intelligence. Where did it get it? If there was only primary and secondary consciousness, where did it come from? You.

How were they given life? Through incidental, creating ideas — ideas. That is all you had to do was to have the idea.

Did you have to fire the engines of genetic evolution? No, all you had to do was have the idea. You see, that is how it works on the Plane of Bliss too, that remarkable place that is detached from the physical. Everything appears immediately as you wish it to be. And can you say it is real? What do you call real? What is the determining factor of reality? Can you touch it, smell it, feel it? Absolutely. You want it to be real, don't you? Well, go jump in the lake, in the lake of tranquillity, and see if there are fish in there. There will be. See if you get wet. You will get wet. See if you can drink the water. You will be able to drink it. See if you can crawl out of the water and get warmed on the grass by the radiant sun. Will you feel the heat? Yes, you will feel the heat. Then is that real? Is this real? Where are you? Aren't you starting to wonder about that now? "Where the hell am I? What am I doing here? Who am I? I don't even know anymore." That is the way you are supposed to think. That is the making of a great initiate. "I don't know where I am anymore. I don't know what is real and so I am going to act like everything is serious business now."

Here is the truth. The truth is that the environment in which you exist is the one to which you have contributed. All of nature around you is a reflection of you because at one point you have made a visitation to it. Now isn't that beautiful? It is like out of our side gushes life, out of our mind gushes ideas that we don't even have to do anything with them. They are the lawgiver to the atomic world. Where does the atomic world get its intelligence? From us who have created it as atmosphere. I am telling you it is so, and it is consistent all the way back up to its Point Zero.

Now here is what I want you to think about. If you get what you deserve because of what you think, then when you are talking to yourself in memory in this light review, there is something you are going to have to remember to say: "My passion, you are to make my passion be a passion of the unknown. I want to belong to the abyss. I want to belong to the potentials. I want to exist in an environment where ideas start manifesting like raindrops around me. I want that because the environment that I come from is already fixed and coagulated. I want a new environment."

The way that you get to dine with masters is you have to think like them. When you start talking about such a lofty concept and then ponder if it is or it isn't, how are you going to convince yourself? You never will, but this day is going to be seen again. That is certain. What perhaps I want to impress upon you is that when you begin to ponder in contemplation these things, there is something wonderful that starts to happen. In contemplation you are becoming analogical mind, the analogical union.

Let's take a look at this from the point of view of my beginning teachings. You are down here at the first plane, living in the carnal Hertzian body. The thoughts we are having today are reserved for great minds that usually exist at the fifth and sixth planes. That means you certainly wouldn't be having that conversation based in the first three seals and that you may be having it in the fourth seal, but more than likely this kind of conversation is going to be happening in the fifth seal and the one back at the base of your head, the sixth seal. If you contemplate why these, it will become self-evident to you.

This is what I want you to understand. If you do have that conversation, then you actually are starting to think on the fifth plane. When you think like we did today, that is how long it takes to go analogical versus try and get that pendulum to stop right here in the Now. That is a mess. You are right up on the sixth plane, the fifth plane, that close. What does that bring you? That brings you right into a rarefied atmosphere again. In primary and secondary consciousness, you don't care about the body because this is not body talk. This is God-Spirit-soul talk and you are right on the fifth plane. When you are, you are brought into a rarefied atmosphere. How many of you today felt that atmosphere in this room? Didn't you start to know something? How many of you were suddenly on the brink of realizing what I was saying? That is the atmosphere and you are coming into it. It gets supercharged.

If you learn to stay in that atmosphere for a while, you are inevitably going to be moving into analogical mind. And if you do, then you are going to be moving into a very changed reality. It is not going to be uncommon that in a moment of talking, suddenly you are going to enter into a tunnel. You will see it and you will look around and you will not be able to see out of your peripheral vision. It will get cloudy. You will look directly at the mist and you will say, "Something is wrong with my eyes." No, you are leaving. You are moving into a rarefied reality. You can get back to this one by rubbing your eyes and insisting on being back here and it will clear up. "Whew, I am glad that passed. I thought there was something wrong with me there for a moment." You want to stay in it because then you are going to start to see flashes of blue and brightly gold-colored lights flashing. When you see them, you are in a rarefied atmosphere. You are on the fifth level. You are in a place where the atmosphere coming off of your mind is going to start manifesting. The abnormal will start to occur as normal. Then is when the master will walk out of the mist because they are already there.

It is at this place of consciousness also that we do the Great Work, the really Great Work, and that we impregnate our life with the atmosphere. We have to live in the atmosphere, this energy, with ideas all around us just pouring off of us. All we have to do is be in it, stay in it. The manifestations will roll off us like sweat, and yet with every drop of sweat there is a realization. There is the precious, aqueous substance that is coagulated thought, that is an adventure, something wonderful and marvelous. That is how we get to a new stratum. People say, well, how do you do this, how do you apply that? Just go back to the principle: Consciousness and energy creates reality. If you can ask the question, if you can beg a greater knowledge, you deserve to live in that knowledge.

In the light, if you can beg to differ with the status quo of the mundane existence and call a halt to the whole show and ask for a reorganization and insist on that reorganization, in the midst of that, then the light and everything else will disappear and the new life will appear as if like a dream, and you will be changed but you will remember the dream. And you will wonder, "Was I dreaming or is this the dream? Where am I? Who am I? What part am I playing here? How have I produced this?" And with that kind of mind, then we start the true evolution.

This also says that then everything — things — have a lineage back to primary consciousness. Everything has a history going back to that momentous moment. In other words, perhaps the alchemist knows more than what is first perceived. Perhaps the alchemist is endeavoring to reach way back to the beginnings to capture the atmosphere, and perhaps the philosopher's stone is captured atmosphere of the seventh plane. And if it is, if it is induced into the electromagnetic body, it will rocket that body back to a seventh-level being and it will preserve it for all time. After all, shouldn't the prima materia be you?

I want you to focus on what you said and wrote to your God today — over and over and over, and go back into sleep with that List.[11] In other words, you are going to start to distort reality here. Sometime when you are lying down, you are going to have to surrender and simply say, "Maybe I am dead. Maybe I really am. So what do I need to do? What do I need to do here

---

11 See also the discipline of the List and Twilight® in the Glossary.

to remedy the situation?" And when you really believe it and you start speaking this, talking directly to yourself, what do you want to say? Because one way or another that speech is going to be revisited in the light. It already has and it is yet to come. If you totally surrender that maybe it has already happened, perhaps with such fortitude, intention, will, and strength, tomorrow morning you may wake up and be born again. So be it.

Our Heart Weighed Against a Feather

O my God,
my days are lengthened,
my soul on fire,
for I am consuming
my past regression.
My soul
is in bloom.
Shine forever,
that that which I am
shall eternally grow
and become the light
of the world.
O my God,
my days are lengthened,
my Spirit is born,
forever
and ever
and ever.
So be it.
To life.

Everything that you do, every thought that you think, should be weighed in the light of all eternity. Every thought, every feeling, should be weighed against a feather. Why? Because the soul sits right here in the chest. Why do you think that the heart sits off to the left of the breastplate? There is a cavity there and a very powerful gland, the thymus. There is where the soul sits. How often have you thought something and had a reaction there? It is interesting trying to explain it because if you have ever analyzed the reaction, when you get the feeling in that place it is the same feeling whether it is guilt, shame, fear, uncertainty, hesitancy. Think about that. Remember this feeling you have had in your chest felt the same way when you were afraid, when you felt guilty, when you were ashamed, or felt bad. It is the same feeling. Who determines the emotional state of this feeling? You do.

When you go against this by thinking something, what you are actually feeling in your chest is what you put together on the Plane of Bliss. On the Plane of Bliss you are viewing a life from the great self, from the God, the Holy Spirit, the soul, the personality. You are viewing it from all different perspectives, and in the total view you get to become the bruising you do to someone else because suddenly you feel the injustice you have done to someone else. You feel that. You feel the pain that you inflict upon others. You feel it first as the self, who feels totally justified in what it is doing, but it also gets to perceive the feeling of the soul the moment that it does it. Its brain is wrestling with its soul — or heart as it used to be called — and it dishes it out. It dishes it out and then it feels justified, so the self is seeing that in the light review. Then the God feels the reaction of it because you create reality. Your job is to create reality. What was the intention and what did the intention deliver and add to the bounty of experience? You get to feel that, so suddenly you feel what happened to the other person. You feel what you have done.

In that review the soul has recorded that and so you take from the whole light review a collection of feelings, subtle energy ideas, intentions, and you have to hold that bag and take a look at it. What you do to others, you do to yourself. You take a look at it and all of that then is recorded, and you walk away from the experience with a mixed bag of goodies because you also see what you do to others. You see your thoughts. When you choose kindness, compassion, and understanding over the rebellious nature of the human being — when you choose to be all parts and you elicit kindness, you elicit understanding to your capacity of understanding — you can say to another individual, "I do not understand thoroughly your experience but I understand part of it and I understand my part in it. I understand what I have given here. Now in the clarity of my being I could have done better. I chose not to. But I do not understand the full impact of what you are going through because that is intimate and personal. That is your path and you set that up on Bliss. Let me correct my part in it — not for you, for me."

When you give understanding, you can be honest and say, "I cannot completely say and admit that I know what it is to walk in your shoes. I do bear wisdom of some things I have observed in you that I own." But you have to own those to see the colors that I see; otherwise it will make no sense to you. They are opportunities. When you do that in life, when you elicit those unsolicited acts of kindness — because you can do something that on the surface appears unsolicited — you always have to check the ulterior motive because that is what you are going to be weighed against. That is how you are seen in the end, and that is the place that you want to be the clearest. Every time that you have gone out of your way and you have helped and been kind without any thought of reward — nothing, just that it is its own reward — every time that you are patient, every time that you are strong in the feeling of weakness, those too are all seen and they are all weighed. You come out from the experience bruised a little bit but feeling good, on the other hand, because your life was in some measure fulfilled in that you made life better for other people because you made it better for yourself. You see, what you have to come to understand is that everything comes back to the ultimate creator, and the ultimate creator of every individual life is you. Why? Because you are the ones who are given the authority of free will and intention, and you get to use that however you see fit, without good or bad.

What is the pain that you suffer? It is the pain that you give to others that hurts you. Your suffering is not about anyone else; it is about your suffering. It is what you have done to you. In that view, everything is weighed, and that unprovoked goodness does not outweigh the provoked intention to destroy, malign, or hurt for the sake of staying alive. So many lives are unjustly lived because they are lived for the sake of survival rather than the Godhead itself. What you do in each life weighs heavier in flaws than in perfection, so that is why every life you keep coming back. You keep going there, reviewing, coming back, and you start building it up until one day you tip the scale where the remarkable good in you outweighs those flaws. That is what you are working for — polishing. Now why? You could go anywhere else; correct? Well, yes. In the whole of the Void and indeed in the whole of the kingdom of heaven, you can go anywhere else. But here is the point that you have to understand. You can only do what you know. You can only go where you know and to what you are attached, and everyone is attached to the imperfection in perfecting it. And for what reason? To be free. Why do you want freedom? Because you want to own this plane and own the rapacious attitudes that seem to go along with culture. You want to own those, where you have none of them inside of you because you have a mission, to make known the unknown. In other words, you are explorers in the Void. You are voyagers to Infinite Unknown.

What kind of God would I be teaching you about if the only end to this life that you could see was a life lived like ordinary people in a mundane situation that had no challenge to it, no adversity, no growth, where every neighbor is trying to protect his or her own? What kind of God would give you such a life? I mean, is that the highest pinnacle of a life's achievement? No, and everyone has already lived that. The highest pinnacle is to address the adversity in life that you are vulnerable to and indeed to make short-order of it because you do not want to be attached to it. If you are attached to it in any sort of prejudice, you are going to be tied in at that moment of weighing yourself in the light.

The remarkable gift is this teaching. It is very profound. It suggests to you that at this moment you know you are looking at you and if not this moment, this moment is going to come. So how do you want to see it? Because this is a bus stop, a train station. It could be utterly possible that it is so, for what proof do you have that it isn't? And don't you have greater aspirations for life? What about all of those dreams that have flitted in and out that have gone unexperienced? How do you get those? By making room for them in your life. How do you do that? By getting unstuck in your life and being so clear that you can entertain an idea and it manifests without being clogged in the plumbing of the mind.

I say to you to think every thought as if it could be written across the sky for everyone to see, think every thought that in a hundred thousand years or a hundred years or five years you would welcome that thought back because it came from a state of honor. There are degrees of evolution. In everything you do, remember, consider doing it in the light of all eternity. What kind of revenge, petty revenge, is worth ten thousand reincarnated lifetimes? I daresay that the cost is just a little too heavy and who is really worth that? No one is. No one is worth missing evolution. That is the train I want you on.

Now in the light review, what happens is that when it is all said and done, then you are stripped of the emotions. They are being fed on by the light because they are polarized emotions. The lords of the light feed on polarized feelings — polarized energy — because that is what light is, and you are stripped of it. You are allowed to go rest and contemplate and are given exactly the most exquisite place that you could ever dream of to be in to do such a contemplation. And in that rest, you have thousands of years — which may seem like an afternoon — thousands of years to ponder, to heal, to ripen, and to get ready to return.

Common Thought Is What Creates Our Daily Life

Now does consciousness and energy on the Plane of Bliss work on the Earth plane? Absolutely, it does. In contemplation at the lake of tranquillity, as you contemplate and view, as you remarkably and daringly become the whole self in any situation, you also become that in every desire. It is not simply a place where you contemplate upon the misdeeds of your life. It is a place where you contemplate upon the dreams of your life, and there you can have long dreams — long dreams — that oftentimes are the greatest healer of all. The dreams can become so impassionate — on the Plane of Bliss impassionate means analogical — that they become so analogical and so impactful that the whole of the being is there and transformed in the midst of the dream itself. And there they may dream dreams, and you have done the same thing, especially when something tells you you can do that.

By virtue of dreaming it on the Plane of Bliss, when the whole self is empowered and it analogically conceives a world, a life, an experience, it is not a matter of are you focusing there as a discipline but that you really are just that. No matter what you do, you are in a state of focus that is very profound and so easy because that is the natural state on Bliss. You do not have a physical body pulling at you to be taken care of, unless you have been so physical that the idea of self cannot be understood unless it is inside of a body. For the most part you are caught up in your spiritual body — beautiful, exquisite body — and it doesn't pull on you. You do not have body problems. Naturally what happens in a state where the self is in contemplation or in a dream is that they are totally in a dream and there is no pull, none, and that is the state on Bliss. How powerful is this? When you come to school and you learn and then I endeavor and beseech you to carry that on into your life, I am endeavoring to get you to accept a state of focus and to be highly protective of the state of focus because whatever sits there as common thought is reality.

Changing the ulterior motives in each of you intentionally helps dramatically alter the anatomy of common thought, because if you are an unhappy person inside, your common thoughts just keep reflecting that. They just keep going out into your life. Now I want you to listen to those thoughts because the seed of their flowering is the ulterior motive. If you are a revengeful person and you have hate in your heart, that is a seed and it flowers common thought from it. Then an everyday exchange has an opportunity to be the flowering of a life. Here you have a flowering of poison, literally. That is the garden. That is the consciousness that is flowering in some of you. Well, that common thought is reality. The idea is that if you can open up your chest, tear out all of the garbage that is in it, burnish those shelves and put one beautiful, brilliant thing there that becomes the ulterior motive, then the flowering of common thought from that will be assured that you will have a magical life and a sweet life, a life that is empowered, that is one with nature instead of warring against it, a life that allows the dream to come about quickly. You know, it is the way you feel light in body, not heavy in body.

On the Plane of Bliss your ulterior motive is not buried — it is on the surface — and from that there is a flowering in long dreams. Those who have the remarkable dreams of the future, so analogical are they — and such a long time are they in that state — that when they incarnate, they seem to have a whole different agenda. They are not normal in the sense that other people are normal. What interests other people may interest them mildly for moments, but you begin to see that the thrust of this individual is much different, marginally different than people who do not come back with great dreams. This becomes their ulterior motive, even as children, and that motive starts to build in their life. They may build up rust and crust just from the harrowing experiences of society and culture, but for the most part so integrated is the dream from Bliss, the desire from Bliss, that it stays right underneath the surface. All common thought that comes from it, though tainted by surface corrosion, is by and large much more powerful. These lives are going to be meaningful lives because the ulterior motive in them is meaningful — meaningful. See it as an innate goal that has been set into place.

When you don't dream those dreams and you are coming back with your mixed bag of things you have to take care of, then those are the ulterior motives that sit inside of you. If you were a harsh entity before, you are going to come back as that again so that you have an opportunity in your harshness to override it and turn it over. You are going to have the exact kinds of individuals in your life as you did the last life because it takes those, who are endeavoring to learn too, for an exchange to occur. Everything in one's life is an opportunity to elevate, is an opportunity to evolve, to change.

Now the soul: You feel the soul here in your chest. Why does it send you those messages? Because what you lay down in the carrier soul when you return is the life plan for this existence. That life plan says, when you finish your contemplation, "I am going to do better." But when the opportunity arises and you fall back into the past patterns, remember that the garbage can outweigh the meaningfulness. You have a lot of garbage in there. If you fall back on that saying, "Well, that is how I am," that is honorable, but now isn't it honorable to say, "This is my opportunity to change that in myself. Do I or don't I want to evolve? Do I want to grow or not? Do I want to partake of a life that I don't have to work so hard anymore in it, that I have laid down the good works in this life that one day I can come back and have clarity and be so unattached but powerful? If I am not finished here, I can't go anywhere else because my business is here. I am too primitive to go anywhere else and too advanced to go somewhere else. I am caught right where I created it to be." Yes, somewhere you have to make up your mind to do the work.

When you go against that, you get this pain right in your chest. If you have felt it, you should listen to it. You should always listen to it because this is a log you laid down on Bliss.

To go against it is to have to repeat it. When do you get tired of doing that? Sometime you have to take a stand and make war and you conquer, bring it on, and sharpen your sword and march. And I don't care, it is a humbling experience, but greatness comes from humbleness. Humble people are daringly bold. They are ostentatious. When you live by this, when you feel fear in your chest — remember, the feelings are all the same — who is saying what this is? You are saying what it is. What are you afraid of? You always have to ask that question: "Why am I afraid? Am I afraid of this confrontation? Am I afraid to be honest? What is the fear that I am feeling here, or is that which I am feeling here being misinterpreted?" Most of the time it is because most people don't like to deal with their own conscience. That is why you have to have the whole self in the light review, because to view it from the self of personality is painful and is difficult. That is the reason why the Observer is standing there, the Holy Spirit is there, that it can be switched with absolute love and support so that what can be seen will not be fearful. Your greatest fear is to make contact with your conscience, and you avoid it. That is what happens.

Now you have returned and are going to return with a bag of goodies. A lot of them just aren't pretty at all, but a lot of them are exquisite. You are beautiful and you know that, and there are parts of you that you love what you are. Maybe the wretchedness of you far outweighs it, but look for a little something. Hold onto it every day and say, "I love this about myself." You know, that is the purposeful good. You have to also put a smile on your face and say, "What is so marvelous about all of this — these troubles that I have in my life and this personality that I have that is so hard to get along with — is that I know that about me. But what I celebrate is that I am so powerful I made me that way, and that is refreshing because I am really on the path to turning it around. I know I had the power to put it there. I know I have the power to erase it." You see? And maybe that is the only little thing that you can find that is sparkling about you, but that is enough.

There are others of you who are going to have just a whole lot of goodness, just a whole, great, long margin of joy, a great margin. That joy is a natural effervescence of someone who has conquered, you know, and there is more of that joy in their life than there is depression. These people have mastered, and that mastery is not about mastering other people; it is about ourselves. They have a natural state of joy that is a little disturbing because it almost smacks that they are really disinterested in your problems, but they are. They really are, and that just fries you. It fries you because you want people to feel sorry for you, and the people that don't, you are not going to cater to them. You want the woe-is-me group. Look around you. If you are a woe-is-me person, look around you. So are they.

Joy is a release and it is also wisdom, and that is what you get when you love yourself enough to tackle your difficulties. To expect someone else to do it for you is meaningless. I, as your Teacher, will not make you happy. I am here to tell you what you are — and you get to make choices from that — and to give you excellent knowledge that you can start to integrate, to give you hope, and to keep reminding you I am talking to Gods out here. I am talking to immortals that are so powerful they can believe themselves into eternal death. That is how powerful you are. I am talking to Gods.

You see, that is what you keep forgetting. This is the pristine message. That is what you are going to know at the light. You were worth coming and taking a second look. Don't you see that? What if you weren't? What if this was it and then you went into the big sleep never to awaken again? This is what you keep forgetting, that you are a divine being. This is so sweet because it means that you exist in the bosom of God and that in there the only condemnation you ever have had is from yourself. And the only reprieval that you will ever get is from yourself. Isn't that the way a sovereign should be? Absolutely.

You Are Gods, the Creators of Reality

When I told you that you may already be dead, you just may be. But what I am here to remind you — and what you are going to hear again and I am going to be telling it to you when you view this life again — is you are a God. You are divine. Remember that. Everything is about choice and opportunity, which is your rightful place in the kingdom of heaven. Although my message seemed to cry out of doom and bewilderment, it was a message worthy for a divine ear. Yes, you are worthy to hear that. That means you are a big person, a big being, and you are to remember that when you hear me again tell you that one blissful moment you are God incarnated and you must choose the path where that Godhead is perceived as total power, total mind, total love, eternalness. You must create a life where that remarkable character can be shining through you at all times. I want you to remember that you have the power to have a life where God is made manifest through you, that the marvelous deeds of a supreme intelligence can be made manifest through you, and that all of the hurt and pain that you have created, you created.

It is never too late to say, "Do I want to keep this game up or to be a marvelous being where the power and love of the Holy Spirit flows through me?" How practical is that in life? It enriches the job you are doing. It shouldn't be a job. It should be an opportunity, a created, embellished opportunity to do better. It is an opportunity in your family to shine, to be unconditional love, to allow truth on every level. It is an opportunity to love your children unconditionally, to live a life where you are a giant in their eyes instead of becoming small, when they are old enough to see your fallacy. It is an opportunity that you live your life in such a way that is remarkable, that they, being given the care of you, are exercising the great stewardship of showing another what it is to be better, to be greater, and to make certain that there is no hidden agenda that the child can see. This is an opportunity to be it to your lover, to your husbandman, to your wife.

When I told you yesterday why you are holding it together, that is more painful than being honest. It takes a great person to love you enough to say no, to love themselves enough to say no. Don't you want someone with substance, true character? That is dependable and that you can count on. They are going to be at your back and by your side because they are worthy people. They are not hypocrites.

Why don't you let it fall apart? To many of you that sounded cruel. Why? Because you are taught to sacrifice, to hold it together? For what, a lie? What kind of fruit does that bear in a relationship? Let it go. I am talking about on any level, wherever this problem is in your life, let it go, shine. So what happens? Everyone packs up and moves. Allow it. You called the shots here. You allow it. Why? Yes, it is emotionally hurtful, but what now is the new ulterior motive? It is honor. It is integrity. That sounds cruel. It sounds selfish. But isn't that what we are talking about here is being in tune with self? Sometimes when you let it go, it is opening a cage and letting a bird fly. You never want to be a prisoner or a jailer because when you are, you are that to yourself. Remember, you are coming back to the acts of the being who stands alone in a light review. You let it go, let it fall apart. And you may fall apart, but there is an ulterior motive here for wellness. You don't have to say anything else. You don't have to excuse. Nothing. "I don't feel anything but healing." That is enough. Anything else is subject to conjecture. How you are going to remold is going to be something that you have to allow to happen and allow yourself to grow according to the ulterior motive there. You always have to make certain that is in place and it is clean.

What happens when you do this? Many things are going to happen. The immature in your life are going to be dross and they are going to go away. Good. Good. It is about time. Let them go. The immature will always be yelping away, snapping and hissing at a distance, "Woe is me, woe is that." Now you get to see what you were holding together. Frightful, isn't it? A little frightening. You let it go because now everything becomes real clear to you or what you let go of is feeling the same thing, and healing starts occurring in everyone's camp. Then what we have is a jump-start in a relationship, whatever that relationship is — it could be you and a butterfly — and you are off and running.

There are always alternatives, but the one that you care about the most is the one you bear yourself. And that is the teaching because I promise you if you say, "I gave up my life and I lived it for this person," what is going to be seen in the light is resentment. That is not love. What you want to do is have an opportunity right now to be magnificent. Every opportunity is magnificent and you get to make a choice. You also have to do something else that is painful. You have to take your sword out and cut the head off of your past. You have to raze it to the ground. Why? Because you want to do it in such a way that you never revisit it again — never, ever. Destroy it, everything about it. You destroy it because you never want to visit it again. I know it has served you. I know your victimization, your tyranny, your pain, your suffering, all that has served you. I know you use it against people to make them feel guilty, ashamed, feel sorry for you. It is all manipulation. It is manipulation. Are you that pitiful that you have to be so wretched to manipulate people? Are you really that pitiful? You see, I see you — and so does your God see you — as a wimp, a noxious wimp. Are you really so pitiful that you have to play games? No, cut it to the bone. That is it, you are born two minutes ago. Two minutes ago you are reborn. That is what I am trying to tell you. This is a light review. You are going to be reborn again. Do you want to go back to your past? Want to go back to that previous life? Going back to your past is going back to a previous life.

Engaging the Life Review Now through the Great Work

I have taught you that you create the atmosphere of each level. There is a school of thought that talks about the transmigration of souls in which starting with a lowly amoeba and a rock, their souls will start to migrate.[12] That is true to a degree because everything is in evolution. And who are the engines of evolution? You are. If the lowly amoeba got its

---

12 The belief in the transmigration of souls is commonly referred to as metempsychosis: the belief in the passing of soul, Spirit, or personality upon death into another body, whether of the same or a different species. The Greek roots of this word are "meta," meaning change, and "psyche," meaning soul. Metempsychosis is another word for reincarnation. This belief was held broadly in all the religions of ancient Greece and the religions of the East. It is a belief that has been held by the majority of people from all cultures in the world throughout history.

haphazard, little start from something you were talking about with your God and off shoots an amoeba, then the amoeba actually represents that conversation.

Remember, all energy waves are carriers of an idea, an intelligence, a thought. That is what common thought looks like. Common thought radiates from you like a central sun. In your bands you radiate common thought, and obviously this little entity is a pretty happy entity so the ulterior motive here is like sunshine. Because that sits at the base of the mindful intelligence of this individual, then common thoughts are moving out into conscious energy potentials and the common thoughts just start spiraling around them. You are just dropping this stuff — here is an amoeba — and you don't even know that you are doing it. Every thought that is radiating out there is doing this and it is spiraling into energy potentials, and that is how you create reality.

When you come to school and you begin your mastership studies, you begin to see that this is what you have always done and that the reason you haven't seen remarkable things in your life is because they are all around you always. It is like a fish wanting a drink of water. What do you say to a fish that says I am thirsty? Well, that is what you begin to understand. It starts to come together. You really start to get a sense of this on the Plane of Bliss, and because everything is already formed around you, you don't see that as miraculous but in fact all of this has been making your reality continuously. If you say, "Why is my life the way it is," then you have to search and find the seed that is causing that to happen.

If we know that common thought is the power manifester, when you come to my school you learn the diligence of discipline, long periods of focused concentration. All disciplines you do here are about creating reality intentionally. You are intentionally doing something that is a natural state to you. But what is so marvelous is that it consists of ideas, thoughts — I give them to you, you start drawing them — that when you intentionally focus on them, they start radiating out of you. That wasn't just there on its own. It wasn't stimulated on its own because your modus operandi is a motive that is sitting there and that the brain is hardwired to think every day. We have just artificially introduced an idea that you haven't thought about. The greatness of this training is that idea manifested in the discipline. Now if that idea had taken hold as an ulterior motive, you would be radiating it every day.

Why did I teach you how to do the List? The List for the sincere student literally became a way to rewire the neuronet and in doing so to rearrange intent, except with most people what began to happen is their intent or ulterior motive is ingrained so strongly that when it comes to different things on the List, they don't believe in it. When they come there, there is the ulterior motive that is not supporting the List, and that also comes spiraling off. It is almost an intentional negation of something wonderful for you. The serious student in this school can look at its List and say, "Now all right. I have been able to manifest these things on my List, and as long as I do it consistently I am radiating that thought out that it is going to happen. Why have certain things on my List not happened?" That is an indicator of what the ulterior motive is, and it is about self-discovery.

What about why haven't you been able to do a remarkable healing? Because you don't believe that. That is the ulterior motive. You can't trust that you can do it when you don't believe it. In other words, you have a house divided against itself. You have an opportunity for the miraculous but you have a decision that is already set inside of you that doesn't believe it, so you can't depend upon Blue Body® work because it isn't the modus operandi in you. What do you do about that? Well, this is the work. You have to say to yourself, "If my card manifested in Fieldwork® and these other things manifested, then I have a state of acceptance for them. If it doesn't, I don't have a state of acceptance, and why?" There is where you have to drag out the ulterior motive, look at it, and say, "Did I get this from the Plane of Bliss?" Yes. Why? Maybe you have set it up not to be healed. Maybe you have set it up to suffer. Maybe you need to suffer. Maybe that is how you set up the whole thing, because no-thing happens to you by accident. Everything is intentional. All common thought is intentional, and sitting by the sea of tranquillity in that beautiful place, contemplation is radiating out of you like the great central sun.

What is that thing that sits there that says you can have this but you can't have that? Is it changeable? Today it is changeable. Tell that to yourself reviewing this moment. "You change this. I am worthy of splendid health. You know why I am going to be worthy of it? Because I love myself and I love my life. I want to love my life throughout, and I just don't have room for anything other than life." You have to look at it that way. What you do then is you switch that out of your List and you put the ulterior motive in there. You change the motive. Instead of "I accept Blue Body® healing," you put in there, "I now accept life. I am worthy of health." Every time you say that and there is a balking in you, you say it a hundred more times until it surrenders. It is easy to do it on the Plane of Bliss without the body. Here it is ingrained and is a program in the body and you have to change the program. This is a part of being a master. The other part is that if you don't, you are always radiating that you are not worthy of life and it undermines everything, and that is the common thought that goes out. Inasmuch as we have a sourpuss sitting up here that is hateful and vengeful, as much as you sit there with terror and anger and malice — look at that — no matter what goes on during the day, you can wake up in the morning and the birds will be singing and you would just as soon they be dead. "Get them out of here." Your child wakes up happy and you don't want to see them, and everything has this ugly little edge to it. That is common thought. What is it? Something sitting there in you. When are you going to get tired of that? Now this is also about joy. God forbid that you would be happy. God forbid you be happy. Don't want you to have one really happy day. "I suffer." Pigeons poop on their heads. This could be a person who is not worthy of life and that radiates, and it is in every little statement, in every action, in every little feeling. It is just that they are dripping with it. Why don't you change that? Just change it. Deal with it.

Then there are people who can't seem to make their fabulous wealth happen. Self-worth is a marvelous thing because worth is an energy exchange, self-worth. There are people that if they don't feel worthy because they are burdened with guilt or shame or something on that order, then when it comes to accepting fabulous wealth, wealth is equal to worth. The lack of self-worth always undermines it. How can you keep saying "I accept my fabulous wealth" when the real core about worth negates that? You know, you have to change that. You have to say, "What am I not worthy of?" Let us not talk of dollars and cents and rubies and gold. What do I not feel worthy about? Who convinced me and what lie did I believe that I had no worth and no value? What did I accept that I keep negating opportunities? You ask yourself that and don't be afraid to know the truth. Don't be afraid to feel what it is. Remember, the most thing you fear is your human conscience. Get into it and find out what did you do that causes you to have such lack in your life. Lack will have nothing to do with money. It will have everything to do with self-esteem. Have you programmed that into this incarnation, that some way your bag is so heavy on this side you don't feel worthy? You have to change that right now because at any moment karma is neutralized. The moment ulterior motive is changed, there is no more karma. It is done. You are not God on a payment plan. It is done. You only have to find the seed right within you.

Now happiness: When you are ready to accept joy, you cannot accept it based upon another person. Indeed you cannot accept joy based on money and cannot accept it based on age and appearance. You must have joy unconditionally without people, places, things, times, and events, because to base it in anything else is to give your power away and your fruitful happiness. You have to learn to be happy with three beans. You have to learn to be happy without anyone in your life. Aren't you good enough to just be alone? Aren't you good enough company? If you are not and you are afraid to be alone, then maybe you should take a look at who you are living with, meaning you. Why don't you enjoy your company? You don't like your thoughts? You don't like what you do? Well, that should be a clear indicator to you that no one will ever make you happy — not your children, not your appearance, your disappearance, not how much money you have. Nothing is going to make you happy if you don't love yourself and come to terms with it, because that is who is going to stand in this light review. To do that is to love God. To do that is to have love for everyone else. To be happy without having to do something constantly and just sit and be mellow with your thought is an extraordinary something. When you are doing something and you are being entertained all the time, your ulterior motive is coated with conversation or the "something." That is what you are radiating out there. To be happy with yourself is to be so clean that the sun comes out. That is when your Great Work is done. Now this isn't mass conversion; it is individual transformation.

These are the remarkable lessons that you are going to hear again. You are going to hear my voice tell you this when you are standing with your Holy Spirit. I want you to remember that. Remember, it is coming again and you are going to hear this again. Perhaps by the time you hear it again, you will have become it and the soul weighs like a feather. How exquisite.

Can you imagine on a human level how that makes me feel? Now you understand what my mission is. Now do you understand why I have such patience with you, why I love you so much? Do you understand why I talk and teach you the way that I do and I don't let you slide away with anything? Because it is going to come around again, and I know when you are standing there, I am going to be with you. You are going to realize that there really is something that just loves you. Your God just loves you, and this messenger really loves you and understands this is going to come again, every word, and every nod from you, and every movement, and everything you feel and don't feel. By the time this comes around again and you are simply that and you are beautiful and you have cleaned your house, we are going to shine together. How do you think I feel? Don't you know? It isn't a matter about believing in me. Listen to what I am telling you. Believe in yourself. That is why I am back here, because every class we do is meaningful, and if it doesn't change you now, it is going to change you. If I don't get to you now, I am going to get to you. Do you understand? Don't be a buffoon and think this won't be remembered. Do not be a buffoon. Do not be so stupid as to think that this is going to be left out in your light review. It is in there.

Think about this for a moment, because now you are getting to understand me and you are getting to think much loftier. You are getting to have thought patterns much greater than that small, little, tiny little life that you have had. You are starting to open up now. Think about this. What if everything you are seeing now you have become? Think about that. How does your conscience feel today? Is it heavy or is it getting lighter? Is it getting lighter? You see, that then is evolution and that is getting those wings unstuck, and you are starting to feel lighter and more effervescent. That radiates out of you. Then what kind of rest period are you going to have after this review? I have given you such knowledge — and I haven't even scratched the surface — to get you to understand how to think and tell you things that are going to be poignant to you that moment that you look at this that are going to turn you. It is like saying to you, I know that you have a choice in picking the body up or going on and you can make another body but sometime you are going to have to come to love this one. You have made it your master. You have given it the power to have dominion over you. But in doing that, you have done it a disservice because you are not there to rescue it when it is in trouble. You don't know how to rescue it and you don't have the power to do it. You don't know how to keep it from aging. You don't know how to keep it well, how to give it peace, tranquillity. You don't know how to do that, and by not being the master of it, you have given it a disservice.

When you are standing there — this will come so quickly — and you said, "Get back into your body," let us pray that you have loved your body enough by that point by being its master instead of its slave and that you are no longer interested in appearances. You are interested in health. You are not interested in appearances so stop blaming your body for getting someone or not getting someone, because it is going to die and be eaten up by the worm.

Triumph Over Death and the Alchemy of Transmutation

When you love yourself enough to go back, then you are going to join a great group of masters because you are going to come back, and that heart is going to start beating, and you are bringing cognizant memory here and power. You can then erase age, you can create glamour, you can become young, old, whatever. You have the power. The thing is, it is the gift that never dies so that you now have a body without loss of knowledge and memory, and you can finish this up and slowly get lighter and lighter and lighter and lighter. And what is a flaw now, you will correct because you are all beautiful. There is no such thing as ugliness in the kingdom of God. And be you judged by God — not by man, not by woman — be you judged by yourself, not others, then that is being absolutely pure and beautiful. Those of you who choose to do that are going to come back so extraordinarily enlightened, and you have seen the other side and you know this is the truth. You know it is. So everything else I have told you is the truth, and you know it is and you are victorious. You have championed death and live life in ultimate freedom. There are no gray areas. There is only ulterior motive. There are others of you that will say, "Ah, no. I know so much now that I want to make my body. I know how to do that now. I know how to make it, and I know how to make it where it won't forget this moment." And you will do that because that is the range of knowledge you are going to have versus those pitiful Christians that go there to the light waiting for Jesus to save them, and then the Buddhists who just go to oblivion — orange oblivion — wing-tips and all.

You are going to have real knowledge to pose about life because life isn't bad. You made this life. All of these marvelous atoms that surround you, look at them, how they fall off of you. They fell off of you in every atmosphere that you have created, in every one of these kingdoms. Just by having a dream and analogically compressing it and moving back impregnates and pulls all of this energy with the idea itself. It is there and its manifestation just falls off of you. Look around you. You are walking in your own stuff. Now that primordial stuff is intelligence and is you. The alchemists want to take the humblest to the greatest. Why do they want to do that? They want to take the humblest. There is nothing more humble than dirt. They want to take dirt and turn it back into its original. They have to go pretty far up the ladder to do that. Look at where they go, the seventh plane. The philosopher's stone is manifested right there in the seventh plane. It actually is multiplied right there, sent back down, sent back up, involution, evolution, and there it is. You see, alchemy is about involution and evolution. It is about the transcendental life of particles into mass, out of mass. How did they know that it is the great arcanum and the great panacea, meaning that it is the cure-all and the elixir of immortality? Because it was conceived on the seventh plane. It is right there with Point Zero, the beginning. How eternal can you get? Their thrust is to take the common to the uncommon, take it all the way back to the moment that we first became analogical. Whatever is existing right there is the philosopher's stone, right there.

Is it possible? Yes, because every particle is made up of particles within itself. They look like waves when they are unwound. What is the philosopher's stone then? You are consuming a substance that has been unwound as an idea you first had as God. You are consuming your consciousness and energy at the level of the seventh plane. What does that do to the body? What does that do to all of the bodies? It is a powerful, radiating force that transforms. The body is no longer subject to time here on this physical plane. It is subject to eternity at Point Zero. It changes the molecular structure of the body and wholly opens the brain. What is it? Think of this: You are going to eat the substance of the first thought. You are eating your own, original thought. You are eating your own idea. You are consuming the first bodies of God. Now you understand an alchemist. A true alchemist will always create the stone. Do you know why? Because what makes a true alchemist is the knowledge of the seven levels. They have to have a Gnostic mind to understand the beginning, Point Zero; the descent, involution; experience, evolution. Alchemists understood that. Furthermore, they also understood that all substance, all things, were a natural fallout of that beginning so that there were levels to particles that contained literally the divine itself.

Yeshua ben Joseph said a most remarkable thing, as long as people understood it — so did Apollonius of Tyana — when he said the kingdom of heaven can be found in a grain of sand or a mustard seed. No one ever explained that adequately but what it meant was in that small of a thing were contained all the heavens. It contained it in atmospheric consciousness and energy. The ideas that exist there, the knowledge that exists there, are contained in a grain of sand.

The alchemists who understood that consciousness and energy creates the nature of reality — and not every one of them understood that, they did not understand energy carrying an idea with it — were the ones who were successful in developing the stone. Why? Because they understood then that dirt is an idea and it is a fallout from heaven. It is a fallout from Point Zero. It is a fallout from the seventh plane, the sixth plane, the fifth plane, the fourth plane. They understood that. They understood then what they needed to do was to take a grain of sand and decay it. Remember when I talked to you about the moment that you die, the Spirit and soul leave the body and decay starts in immediately. Rigor mortis happens within minutes or hours. That is how fast decay happens. Move away from something that you love and then return within two weeks, there is a decay that has gone on in your absence, a decay. Why? Because you hold things together. When you leave, when the Spirit leaves the house, the house starts to decay. What is decay? It is simply the unraveling.

Now in a grain of sand, alchemists knew that they had to decay the grain of sand. In other words, they had to get it to decay so that the grain of sand molecularly started to fall apart and each molecule containing those particles also started to separate. In the separation, each one of those particles were unraveling inside of a molecule that itself is breaking up, and along with it is coming the idea. At first the intent has to leave a grain of sand. The intent has to leave it, and a master can make the intent leave a grain of sand. When the intent goes — look at it this way — the Spirit has left it, and what they were after was the Spirit escaping. You are after the Spirit escaping because the Spirit escaping is the idea. In its liquefaction, what used to be solid is in liquid flux. It is decaying so it is coming apart. It is just like a caterpillar in a chrysalis, where the Spirit that holds the caterpillar together has left and there is a new Spirit. It is called the butterfly. In the decay of a particle of sand, it goes together in a liquid form and all of this free energy is moving around in it. All that the alchemists have to do is keep decaying this out of the different levels of energy. In other words, they are taking this little grain of sand and are going up with it with heat. Remember heat? What is heat? It is nothing more than the friction of energy in atmosphere. With heat they change its atmosphere. That is the way it works. With continual change, what happens then is this little particle of sand finally gets changed all the way up to where its nucleus is starting to come apart in its atomic structure. As soon as you can get the nucleus to come apart, then you take the "eggs" inside of the nucleus and let those dissolve. You keep releasing, keep getting the Spirit out of even the quarks that are inside of them and dissolve them. Quarks are not going to dissolve until about the fifth plane. When they come out, they have their whole energy, their whole short energy that belongs to the fifth plane. From there, the alchemists are going to relax them until they get them up to the sixth plane and right to the seventh plane.

When you get a grain of sand to relax all the way back to the beginning of its idea, you have opened up the idea of the seventh plane and the seventh body. You are right next to Point Zero, and that is sheer immortality. When you feed that and consume that into a physical body, it does exactly what it is supposed to do. The idea turns back on the giver and restores the brain of the original giver. That means the subconscious comes alive because in it has the exact moment that idea came into being, and it is activated. You then have a body whose vibratory rate is extraordinary and it is going through a metamorphosis. It is being dissolved slowly into the immortal, and it will always be beautiful.

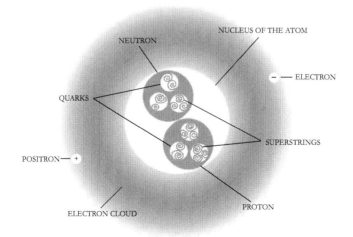

CLOSING WORDS:
LIVING AS MULTIDIMENSIONAL BEINGS

"Perhaps it is time you got in there and saw what you have been afraid to see and start to change it. If you do, you will understand the Plane of Bliss, and this life — this life — can be the Plane of Bliss. Remember, you have an opportunity to be a linear-thinking God or a multidimensional one. I would say go for it on every level."

— Ramtha

Great masterful people are extremely compassionate beings, as you can imagine. They are heavy-laden with wisdom — heavy-laden with wisdom. Imagine for a moment how they must think. You got a taste of it with this teaching, what is on their mind. Well, what is on their mind is their ulterior motive. It is always their motive, and it can be as vast as the Void at midnight. It will never be small. It will be lofty and progressive. They have come by this way and with their heavy-laden wisdom there is often a temptation to help ignorant people. But they also have wisdom that teaches them that ignorant people carry the baggage of victimization and helping them sometimes can be the greatest hindrance. It becomes harder trying to help someone who only sees life as a victim because they consider any help making life difficult for them.

What kind of important insight do you need when you are working with people? You have to be able to see their thoughts and their intent and see all the potentials that come off of them. You have to be able to know their soul, read their thoughts, and understand who needs help and who doesn't. Obviously everyone needs it but not everyone is mature enough to get it. Not everyone, as it were, is ready to advance in their life. That is the reason why so many people are so closed-minded and so lazy. They would rather have someone else think for them than to do it themselves.

Not everyone will understand this message. Not everyone will understand it because they cannot fathom anything other than a linear mind. They cannot fathom the split picture happening simultaneously. They cannot possibly imagine that it has already happened and they are reviewing it and that the next set of occurrences and enlightenment will be that if that is so, then I can change it in any moment. They can't think that way. They only think linearly, up and down, born, dead, back and forth. They cannot think in multiple ways. A dimensional mind is exactly what a master must have because a master knows they are consciousness and energy. Why would they choose a linear path? Why wouldn't they choose all paths simultaneously? Interesting concept, isn't it? Instead of becoming, they have already become. And to be able to see all potentials simultaneously, how do they do that? They made it their intent to do that. Just as you make it your intent to be a certain way, their intent is to know all things, and they get it. What is going to stop them? Isn't creating reality equal to what you can dream? Isn't it equal to that which is termed the level of knowledge which one possesses? It is the difference between a child dreaming and an adult dreaming. As we gather more information and more data, it broadens our horizons. This teaching is endeavoring to do that, but you have to know that lofty beings think lofty thoughts. They think them in just the same way. This moment, in the light of all eternity, I exist. How shall I shine? What sorts of benefits do I want to come back to me? What path do I want to walk, because the path that I walk will be sprinkled with the sand of my consciousness. Is that going to be a prickly path? Is it going to be a dangerous path? Are the sands that you walk upon — the ideals that are coagulated underneath your feet, that saffron dust — are those explosive particles? Are they poisonous particles? Are they dangerous particles? Are they ideas of love, opportunity, and unlimitedness? How is your path coagulated? You cannot walk on anyone else's path. The very ground you walk on, you change. The very path, the very day-to-day existence in your life, is made up of your own consciousness, so when you are unraveling that bit of sand and taking it back to the seventh level, you can bet there is going to be some rocky road ahead because of the way you laid it down.

From this day forward, take a look at where you are standing, take a look at what surrounds you. What is the glue that holds that cabin together? What is the mind force in those things around you? Were they built upon a consciousness whose seat was anger? What was their ulterior motive, because that is coagulated in the stuff around you and the stuff you are standing on. Think about it. It is how a master thinks. A master would not walk on any ground but its own. It won't walk on any ground but its own. Remember, the moment you leave your house, it starts to decay. Think about that. If someone comes in and fixes it up, it is their energy they fix up. How could an enlightened being stand on the ground of a reality of anyone else except themselves?

Now you begin to understand those mysteries about those masters that walked the path of saffron dust. The creatures are adored by them and they lie down at their feet. The birds land upon them and flowers bloom where they walk. Those masters walk the path of healing, and whoever follows right behind them is healed, just stepping on the same ground they stepped on. It is because the ground is them. You are not separated from your environment. Your environment is the coagulated force of common thought.

Where do you get the idea that a place is haunted? Isn't there truth to that wives' tale or husbands' tale? It is true that earthbound Spirits, people who are very carnal individuals, do not have knowledge except live day to day for their bodies. They cannot fathom themselves without the body because the body was every bit their consciousness. It was their path, and yet it is into rot now and decay. They are earthbound and they stay within the areas where they have energy. They stay in the atmosphere, they stay in the place they occupy, because that is where they are grounded. Also, the ground in which they were grounded at continuously replays an energy. What is a vaporous vision? Indeed, what is it that sometimes in the vapor rising off certain pieces of ground you can see a faint image? You know why? Because that ground was made up of that common thought.

There is much to be said then about the American Indian or the South American Indian who believed that Spirits of their grandfathers live in the mountains, or Spirits of their mothers upon the prairies, or that the great chiefs gather in some canyon or some mountaintop, or the Spirit of the great buffalo still exists. Why would they have that idea? Because the spiritual energy has made that place what it was. That is why it is sacred. That is why they can go and powwow in that place and sit upon the very ground of intense common thought and receive the energy of their elders. It is a truth.

Why wouldn't it be a truth? How else is the stuff of matter made, by accident? No, there are no accidents in God's kingdom. There is only intention. What makes a holy place? A holy thought. The field in this school is a holy place. This arena, the Great Hall, is a holy place because you have sat here and you have done the Great Work here. If this had been a great arena of great tragedies, you would be sitting in sorrow and you would feel it. Why? Because the particles that are in slow decay are oozing with the energy of that sorrow. That is why sometimes in destroying your past, that is exactly what you need to do. You need to unfurl that which is termed the energy and let it rot, let it go back, and let it be purified. Purification by fire is a long ritual of burning a place of sorrow, of burning a place of memory, of burning a haunt. What is burning doing? It creates the internal sulfur of the wood itself to ignite and unravel, and the common thought goes up in smoke. That is the reason why in doing Consciousness & Energy® work, you do not wear jewelry while you are focusing — particularly metals having to do with the past — because the past is looped into the energy. Metal is perhaps the greatest retainer of consciousness and energy there is. That is why gold is given in friendship and love, and when the feeling is no longer there it should be taken off and melted down, because otherwise if you continue to wear it, you are continuously getting fed a thought.

Does this mean that you go home and set brush fires? I don't want you to do that. I want you to understand that sometimes maybe that invisible depression you are feeling is the place where you are standing, the room you are in, something that is around you and it is feeding back to you, and that needs to be taken care of by you. Remember, you cannot stand on any ground that has not been affected. All ground is affected. Masters create their own path. I ask you to do that because to see wherever you step and wherever you go simply to be the extending environment of your choice is still an immature master. It is an immature student. Understand the effect is everywhere and that the fallout of common thought is coagulating all of the time.

Think about how many times you have had a room that has nearly been hermetically sealed and you come back and there is dust. Where did it come from? It is your thoughts coagulating in the room or it is the room in decay. You don't have to have any source for it to come in. It will just come of itself. It is in the atmosphere. We are talking of layers of magic here. What happens then when you create a change in the ulterior motive? Then you start broadcasting common thought and it just starts manifesting around you. When masters don't want dirt on their garments, because that is not where it belongs, it never gets there. When masters walk lightly on their path, it is because their common thought is light, common thought. When masters seemingly have a seamless life, it is because they made it that way. It seems that no matter what they do, they do it well and things always work out for them. That is because that is the way they made it. That is because they fundamentally think that way and everything within their orbit is wound up in such thinking.

This should be very impactful for you. You should go home and take a look at what depresses you and take a look at where you are. What is stored in the fabric around you, what kinds of thoughts? They should be changed. Furthermore, you should remember to remind yourself that when you do Create Your Day® dutifully, as you have been taught to do, that this is how you are creating it and that day becomes the fallout of this common thought — an intentional, common thought.

You are not at the place at this very moment that you simply wake up and start thinking like a master. You are in the habit of thinking, "Oh, my God, it is morning and the hour, it is late, and I wish to sleep longer." You see, you are not in the habit of opening your eyes and by the time you have opened them you have already created half of your day just by the way that you think. You have to discipline yourself to create those common thoughts of creating your day exactly the way you want it, and it is like magic. Why? Because the fallout is happening through common thought coagulating as your path, as your day itself.

What couldn't you include in it? If your intention is to have a marvelous day, a magical day, a healing day, an energetic day, a miracle day, that is the common thought you have to radiate and that day will give you exactly that. It works every time, unless of course you have sitting there some wretched ulterior motive that is going yeah, yeah, yeah, yeah. You have to get rid of those things. Then the day has the fallout of the miraculous and God does not disappoint you.

What about this life? It is the fallout from the Plane of Bliss. What about this light review? It is the fallout from your life. What about this review? It will be remembered. What do you get from it? All the advantages of extended wisdom, opportunity, choice, and change. Now what you do with that is entirely up to you because you are the Lord God of your being, a sovereign. But never let a day be wasted. It is precious life, one day closer to eternity. And, remember, speak all things and think all things by the measuring stick of the light of all eternity. When you do, you will have learned the rule of the masters and your life will be richer, happier, more joyful, more peaceful, more comfortable, beautiful, and wonderfully predictable. When you are living that way, there is nothing to be afraid of.

Moreover, if this teaching has taught you about ulterior motive and your intention, and you understand that the greatest fear that you have in your chest is confronting your own conscience, perhaps it is time you got in there and saw what you have been afraid to see and start to change it. If you do, you will understand the Plane of Bliss, and this life — this life — can be the Plane of Bliss. Remember, you have an opportunity to be a linear-thinking God or a multidimensional one. I would say go for it on every level. And you live this day multidimensionally and you live it in such a way that it can be viewed over and over and over as if this day is the day you are viewing it and how do you want it lived. So be it.

I love you. I will see you in the light.

O my beloved God,
give I thanks greatly
for this review.
And of this life,
I do cherish and honor.
O my beloved God,
I desire clarity
and adventure.
Free my life
from my illusions,
that my adventure
may begin.
So be it.

EPILOGUE: AN INTRODUCTION TO RAMTHA'S TEACHINGS — KNOWLEDGE, EXPERIENCE, AND WISDOM

The teachings of Ramtha are a unique, metaphysical system of thought. They address the fundamental questions about human existence, the human person, our destiny and origins, the nature of good and evil, the soul, death and life, the world, and our relationship to others.

The format in which Ramtha's teachings are conveyed is intrinsic to the message itself. The teachings are not simply an intellectual dissertation on specific subjects or a mere intellectual analysis of them, nor are they a form of revealed truth that requires the blind allegiance of faith. Ramtha's teachings are not a new religion nor are they the building blocks of a new church. His teachings are a system of thought that contain within their approach to reality the elements and mechanisms that allow the individual to engage Ramtha's philosophy and verify and experience its content firsthand. In other words, this unique aspect of the teachings allows the philosophy, or the *concepts of reality*, to be experienced and become instead *wisdom about the nature of reality*.

This particular quality of Ramtha's teachings resembles the initiations into sacred knowledge practiced by the ancient mystery schools of Greece, Egypt, and the Middle East, as well as the ancient Gnostic schools of the Middle East and Europe. It is important to note that this characteristic distinguishes Ramtha's teachings from the traditional, philosophical schools of the western world.

What we find in the traditional, western understanding of objective knowledge and truth is a fundamental assumption about the human person and the nature of reality. The scientific method limits its range of attainable knowledge to phenomena that can be observed and verified through the senses of the physical body. Anything outside this range is consigned to the realm of myth and folklore. In other words, the nature of reality and the human person are nothing more than its physical nature and materiality. Sigmund Freud's psychoanalysis and profile of the human psyche are a clear example of this trend.

The physical body and the material world, in Ramtha's thought, are only one aspect of the real world. In fact, they are only the product and effect of the real world constituted by consciousness and energy. The human person is best described as consciousness and energy creating the nature of reality, a creator, a divine being. The physical world is only one of seven levels of expression of consciousness and energy. Ramtha uses the concept of the Observer from quantum physics to explain his understanding of consciousness and energy. He also uses the concept of God as creator and sovereign to describe the human person as consciousness and energy.

It can be easy for many people with different cultural backgrounds to dismiss Ramtha's teachings straightaway due to the unusual way in which they are conveyed through channeling, a term he coined when he first appeared in the late 1970s. This unique form in which Ramtha delivers his teachings is by no means arbitrary and superficial. He has pointed out explicitly the reasons behind such a format and explained that in order to grasp his message, it is important to become aware of the roots of our preconceived ideas, unconscious prejudices, and molds in which we normally perceive, judge, and evaluate reality.

Ramtha's teaching techniques often seek to challenge the

individual as well as offer them the tools to become aware of those preconceived ideas that shape and set the boundaries in which we normally perceive reality. The purpose of this is to allow, as a result, the emergence of a broader perspective of mind, which would enable us to experience reality in a more meaningful, unlimited, conscious, and extraordinary way. It also provides us with a greater spectrum of potentiality for our personal experience than was previously available to us by our own judgment.

Ramtha, in presenting his philosophy as the fruit of his own truth and personal experience, makes the point that he is the embodiment of the philosophy, the living representation and manifestation of his teachings. Ramtha consistently explains with his teachings how he can claim that he is an immortal God, consciousness and energy, and that he lived once as a human being 35,000 years ago in the long-gone continent of Lemuria and never died. Ramtha describes how in that lifetime he addressed the questions about human existence and the meaning of life, and that through his own observation, reflection, and contemplation he became enlightened and conquered the physical world and death. He teaches that he realized a way in which to take his body with him to a level of mind in which his true essence as consciousness and energy could remain fully conscious, be completely free and unlimited to experience any and all aspects of creation, and continue to make known the unknown. Ramtha refers to this process as his ascension.

The fact that he is no longer limited by his physical body allows his consciousness and energy to interact with the physical world in other forms. He often refers to himself as being the wind, for example, or the morning, or a stranger, or a beggar on the street observing civilizations come and go, or as anything that consciousness would dare to imagine.

Ramtha uses the body of JZ Knight exclusively to channel and teach in person. A channel is different from a medium in that the channel is not the intermediary between the consciousness coming through it and the audience. The channel does not remain in a transfixed, altered state while channeling but leaves its body completely and allows the consciousness coming through to have full faculty over its body.

Ramtha's choice to channel his message through a woman, rather than by using his own physical body, is making a powerful statement that God and the divine are not the prerogative of men alone but that women have always been worthy expressions of the divine, capable of genius and being God realized. It is also asserting that what is important is not the worshiping of the messenger or a face or an image but to listen to the message itself. It is also making the statement that our true essence as human beings is not limited to the physical body or a specific gender. The phenomenon of channeling, as it happens in JZ Knight, is deeply connected and best understood within Ramtha's view of the nature of reality. Proof of the authenticity of this unique phenomenon therefore would also imply the validity and truth of Ramtha's teachings. This is an important point to consider because science has developed tests and equipment that can scrutinize this phenomenon and study it from a physiological, neurological, and psychological point of view. Scientific techniques now exist to rule out the possibility of fraud. JZ Knight is one of the only channels — if not the *only* one — who has opened herself to such scientific scrutiny. These scientific studies took place in 1996 when a distinguished panel of eighteen scholars — comprised of scientists, psychologists, sociologists, and religious experts — studied the school and JZ Knight before, during, and after channeling Ramtha several times.

The team of researchers was composed of experts from such diverse institutions as Chicago Theological Seminary, Temple University, Colgate University, the University of California, the University of Oregon, Saybrook Graduate School & Research Center, and Birkbeck College at the University of London: Basil Hiley, Ph.D., from Birkbeck College at the University of London; Joscelyn Godwin, Ph.D., from Colgate University; Robert L. Moore, Ph.D., from Chicago Theological Seminary; Susan Jean Palmer, Ph.D., from Concordia University, Quebec, Canada; Constance A. Jones, Ph.D., from Graduate Theological Union, Berkeley, California; Joseph Bettis, Ph.D., from the Northwest Research Group; Stanley Krippner, Ph.D., Ian Wickramasekera, Ph.D., Judy Wickramasekera, Ph.D., and Charles Winstead, III, Ph.D., from Saybrook Graduate School & Research Center; Franklin H. Littell, Ph.D., and Marcia Sachs Littell, Ph.D., from Temple University; J. Gordon Melton, Ph.D., then Director of the Institute for the Study of American Religions of the University of California, Santa Barbara; Amit Goswami, Ph.D., from the University of Oregon; Gail M. Harley, Ph.D., Professor of Religious Studies from the University of South Florida, Tampa; Carroll Adam Cobbs, M.S., and Charles LeWarne, Ph.D., retired Professor of History from the University of Washington; and John Simmons, Ph.D., from Western Illinois University.

After they conducted their scientific research studies, using the latest psychological and medical tests, technology, and equipment available at the time, they concluded that the readings taken from JZ Knight's autonomic nervous system responses were so dramatic that they categorically ruled out any possibility of conscious fakery, schizophrenia, or multiple-personality disorders.

Ramtha initiates his students into the knowledge so that they may personally experience what they are learning and turn it from mere theory or philosophy into wisdom. These initiations take the form of various disciplines of his design where the student has the opportunity to engage the teachings. Ramtha differs from other teachers in this aspect. He takes on the role of a Master Teacher and Hierophant, a teacher who has the power to manifest what he speaks and intends, a Teacher who is equipped to initiate his students. This is an important aspect of the teachings that likens Ramtha's School of Enlightenment to the Gnostic movement and the ancient mystery schools. Nevertheless, a close examination of Ramtha's teachings shows a clear distinctiveness in form and content from what is traditionally known as Gnosticism and the philosophy of the mystery schools. Ramtha does not refer to his teachings in these terms. Rather, he calls it Ramtha's School of Enlightenment, the School of Ancient Wisdom, dedicated to the Great Work. The Great Work is the practical application of Ramtha's teachings where each student has the opportunity to apply the knowledge and turn it into personal experience. The students of the Great Work have the opportunity, in this setting of the Mystery Schools, to know themselves and become enlightened.

Ramtha's teachings cover a vast amount of subjects, yet they all serve to expound the fundamental concepts of his own system of thought. On repeated occasions he emphasized that the totality of his message could be expressed in the statement, "Behold God. You are Gods." But how are we to interpret this statement? There are probably as many definitions of the term God as there are people on Earth. In order to understand Ramtha's teachings correctly, it is crucial that we become aware of both our own concept of God and how it stands in contrast with Ramtha's explanation and definition of God and the nature of reality.

What is the essence of all things? What is their source? What is their nature? What is their destiny? Ramtha's approach to these questions begins with his concept of the Void. The Void is the Source from which all that exists sprang. He describes the Void as "one vast nothing materially, yet all things potentially." In the Void there is nothing — neither movement nor action. Many philosophical approaches to the question of God, including the theologies of monotheistic religions, have conceived of God as an all-knowing, infinite, absolute, transcendent, and immutable being. In Ramtha's system, the attributes of absoluteness, infinity, and immutability are characteristics of the Void. The Void is self-contained, self-sufficient, in a state of rest, and no need. Even though the Void is seen as an all-encompassing vastness, in its original state it contains no knowledge of itself, for knowledge is an action.

The concept of God as creator — "first cause" and "unmoved mover" that we find in Aristotle's philosophy and Thomas Aquinas' theology — is described by Ramtha in terms of the Void contemplating itself and knowing itself. This act of contemplation represents a unique movement in the Void that produced a point of awareness and knowingness of itself. This point of awareness is referred to as Point Zero, the Observer, primary consciousness, consciousness and energy, and God. Point Zero carries the primordial intent to make known and experience all that is unknown and in a state of potentiality within the vastness of the Void. This is the basis for evolution. The Void contemplating itself is the Source and origin of the human person. Ramtha's statement, "You are God," refers to the person as the Observer, the embodiment of Point Zero, and creative consciousness and energy.

Point Zero fulfilled its nature to make known the unknown and evolve by imitating the act of contemplation of the Void. In doing this, Point Zero produced a reference point of awareness that served as a mirror through which it could become aware of itself. Ramtha refers to this mirror consciousness as secondary consciousness. Point Zero rests in the bosom of the Void and has no limits to what it can know. The reflection between Point Zero and the mirror consciousness is what produces an environment, a tangible plane of existence in time and space. The Spirit is the dynamic aspect of Point Zero. It is the will or intent that desires to know and experience the unknown. The exploration of the potentials of the Void by Point Zero and the mirror consciousness is what produced seven levels of consciousness and, correspondingly, seven levels of time and space, or frequency. This journey and act of creation down seven levels of consciousness and energy are referred to as the journey of involution. The journey back to God and the Void is called the journey of evolution. The soul is different from the Spirit. Ramtha speaks of the soul as the Book of Life. The soul is the recorder of all the experiences and the wisdom gained in the journey of involution and evolution.

The predicament of the human being is expressed in terms of forgetfulness, amnesia, and ignorance of its origins and destiny. The traveler, or mirror consciousness, identified itself so much with the densest and slowest plane of existence that it forgot its own immortality and divinity. Humanity has become a stranger to itself, to the God that lives within us and is us, and has searched for help, meaning, and redemption from an outside source. In doing this, humanity denies its own divinity and precludes any chance for liberation from its present condition.

It is important to note that in Ramtha's teachings, the material world — the densest plane of existence — and the physical body are never regarded as evil, undesirable, or intrinsically bad. A dualistic interpretation of reality typically found in the Gnostic traditions — emphasizing the struggle between good and evil, good and bad, light and darkness, Spirit and matter, sin and righteousness — is intrinsically excluded in Ramtha's teachings. What becomes an undesirable condition is to remain in a state of ignorance and denial as to our true nature and destiny. It is absurd to argue for our limitations when we are, as consciousness and energy, the ones who created them.

The path to enlightenment is the journey of evolution back to Point Zero. In accomplishing this task, the person fulfills the mandate to make known the unknown and bring to the Void its experience to be turned into perennial wisdom.

All of the disciplines of the Great Work designed and used by Ramtha to initiate his students are modeled according to, and imitate in some way, the process of the Void contemplating itself, which gave birth to consciousness and energy, which in turn creates the nature of reality.

In conclusion, the four cornerstones of Ramtha's philosophy are the concept of the Void, consciousness and energy creating seven levels of reality, the statement, "You are God," and the mandate to make known the unknown and to conquer yourself. There are many traces of Ramtha's teachings found in ancient traditions, although in most cases all that remains are faint echoes that have barely survived the passing of time and have lost their appropriate context for interpretation. Some of these traditions are the philosophies of the ancient Egyptians and Pharaoh Akhenaten; Buddha's description of himself as the awakened; Socrates' understanding of virtue and the immortality of the soul; Plato's concept of universal forms; Yeshua ben Joseph's life and teachings; the works of St. Thomas the Apostle and his *Hymn of the Pearl*; the hymn to the divine word in the Gospel according to John; the life and teachings of Apollonius of Tyana; Origen; Mani; Francis of Assisi; the Jewish and Christian mystics; John of the Cross' sketch of *The Ascent of Mount Carmel*, where the apex is placed at the top of the head of the human body; the works of art of various artists like Michelangelo and Leonardo da Vinci; the writings and mystical experiences of Therese of Avila; the works of Fray Luis de Leon; the Cathars and Albigensians; the humanists of the Renaissance movement in Europe; the Rosicrucians; the masters of the Far East; and many others.

The teachings of Ramtha offer us a unique perspective from which to view the mystery of life. They offer us a framework in which the questions that have remained unanswered by philosophy, science, and religion find a new meaning. These teachings can broaden the scope of human experience far beyond the boundaries set by science and the various religions of the world to this day. Ramtha's teachings are neither a religion nor a philosophical interpretation of reality. They are the truth that was gained and verified by the experience of a member of the human race. In this sense they are Ramtha's knowledge, Ramtha's science, and wisdom. And now that the path has been trodden upon, the doors are open for those who desire to explore it and make their own journey into the unknown.

— *Jaime Leal-Anaya*
Editor and Writer, JZK Publishing

Sources

The chapters of this book were constructed from various live Ramtha events on the subject that took place over several decades. *Chapter I: The Wheel of Reincarnation* was taken from Ramtha Dialogues® Audiotape 268, *The Plateau for Learning,* November 7, 1989; and Ramtha Dialogues® Audiotape 336, *Only One Thing,* September 19, 1996.

Chapter II: The Art of Detachment and Unconditional Love was taken from Ramtha Dialogues® Audiotape 336, *Only One Thing,* September 19, 1996.

Chapter III: The Last Battle against Tyranny and Slavery, was taken from Ramtha Dialogues® Audiotape 302, *Update on Change,* January 9, 1991.

Chapter IV: Redefining the Self As the Spiritual Self, and *Chapter V: Making the Choice That Endures into Eternity* were taken from Ramtha Dialogues® CD-9703 and CD-9703.1, *Plane of Bliss I — On Earth As It Is In Heaven: Our Journey Through Life, Death, and Beyond,* January 24-26,1997.

Chapter VI: Death and the Revelation of Our Ulterior Motive, Chapter VII: When You Love Yourself Enough, and *Closing Words: Living As Multidimensional Beings,* were taken from Ramtha Dialogues® CD-9716, *The Plane of Bliss II,* August 8-10, 1997.

RAMTHA'S SELECTED GLOSSARY
OF TERMS AND DISCIPLINES

For more information on Ramtha's teachings, his disciplines and techniques for personal transformation and focus, please visit or write to Ramtha's School of Enlightenment, P.O. Box 1210, Yelm, WA 98597, U.S.A., www.ramtha.com. Ramtha's book, *A Beginner's Guide to Creating Reality,* Third Edition (JZK Publishing, 2004), contains Ramtha's introduction to his teachings, his disciplines, and his School of Enlightenment.

Analogical Mind: Being analogical means living in the Now. It is the creative moment and is outside of time, the past, and the emotions.

Bands, the: The bands are the two sets of seven frequencies that surround the human body and hold it together. Each of the seven frequency layers of each band corresponds to the seven seals of seven levels of consciousness in the human body. The bands are the auric field that allow the processes of binary and analogical mind.

Binary Mind: This term means two minds. It is the mind produced by accessing the knowledge of the human personality and the physical body without accessing our deep subconscious mind. Binary mind relies solely on the knowledge, perception, and thought processes of the neocortex and the first three seals. The fourth, fifth, sixth, and seventh seals remain closed in this state of mind.

Blue Body®: The body that belongs to the fourth plane of existence, the bridge consciousness, and the ultraviolet frequency band. The Blue Body® is the lord over the lightbody and the physical plane. It is also a discipline taught by Ramtha in which the students lift their conscious awareness to the consciousness of the fourth plane. This discipline allows the Blue Body® to be accessed and the fourth seal to be opened for the purpose of healing or changing the physical body. This technique is taught exclusively at Ramtha's School of Enlightenment.

Body/mind consciousness: Body/mind consciousness is the consciousness that belongs to the physical plane and the human body.

Book of Life: Ramtha refers to the soul as the Book of Life, where the whole journey of involution and evolution of each individual is recorded in the form of wisdom.

Consciousness & Energy® (C&E®): "The breath of power." Consciousness & Energy® is the service mark of the fundamental discipline of manifestation and the raising of consciousness taught in Ramtha's School of Enlightenment. Through this discipline the students learn to create an analogical state of mind, open up their higher seals, and create reality from the Void. A Beginning C&E® Workshop or Class 101 is the name of the introductory workshop for beginning students in which they learn the fundamental concepts and disciplines of Ramtha's teachings. The teachings of the Beginning C&E® Workshop can be found in *Ramtha, A Beginner's Guide to Creating Reality,* Third Ed. (Yelm: JZK Publishing, a division of JZK, Inc., 2004.) This technique is taught exclusively at Ramtha's School of Enlightenment.

Create Your Day®: Discipline created by Ramtha for raising consciousness and energy and intentionally creating a plan of events and experiences for the day very early in the morning before the activities of the day begin. This technique is taught exclusively at Ramtha's School of Enlightenment.

Fieldwork®: This is one of the fundamental disciplines of Ramtha's School of Enlightenment. The students are taught to create a symbol of something they want to know and experience and draw it on a paper card. These cards are placed with the blank side facing out on the fence rails of a large field. The students blindfold themselves and focus on their symbol, allowing their body to walk freely to find their card through the application of the law of consciousness and energy and analogical mind. This technique is taught exclusively at Ramtha's School of Enlightenment.

JZ Knight: JZ Knight is the only channel through whom Ramtha has chosen to deliver his message. Ramtha refers to JZ as his beloved daughter. She was Ramaya, the eldest of the children given to Ramtha during his lifetime.

List, the: The List is the discipline taught by Ramtha where the student gets to write a list of items they desire to know and experience and then learn to focus on it in an analogical state of consciousness. The List is the map used to design, change, and reprogram the neuronet of the person. It is the tool that helps to bring meaningful and lasting changes in the person and their reality. This technique is taught exclusively at Ramtha's School of Enlightenment.

Mother/Father Principle: It is the source of all life, the Father, the eternal Mother, the Void. God the creator is seen as Point Zero and primary consciousness, which came out of the Void. The Source is the Void itself.

Neighborhood Walk®: Discipline created by JZ Knight for raising consciousness and energy to intentionally modify our brain's neuronet and preestablished patterns of thinking that we no longer desire and to replace them with new ones of our own choice. This technique is taught exclusively at Ramtha's School of Enlightenment.

Sending-And-Receiving: Discipline created by Ramtha to develop the brain's innate ability for telepathy and remote-viewing, both with a specific target or a partner, anywhere, anything, or any time, past, present, or future.

Seven Levels of Consciousness and Energy: The seven levels of consciousness and energy is Ramtha's model of reality and it explains our origins and destiny. It is expressed graphically as a triad, with the seventh level at the top and Point Zero at

the apex. Consciousness and energy are inextricably combined and the seven levels of consciousness correspond to the seven levels of the electromagnetic spectrum. They also represent levels of energy, frequency, density of mass, space, and time. The levels or planes of consciousness and their energy from the first to the seventh are:
1. Subconsciousness and Hertzian
2. Social consciousness and infrared
3. Awareness and visible light
4. Bridge consciousness and ultraviolet blue
5. Superconsciousness and x-ray
6. Hyperconsciousness and gamma
7. Ultraconsciousness and Infinite Unknown.

Seven Seals of Consciousness and Energy: The seven seals are powerful energy centers that constitute seven levels of consciousness in the human body. The bands are the way in which the physical body is held together according to these seals. In every human being there is energy spiraling out of the first three seals or centers. The energy pulsating out of the first three seals manifests itself respectively as sexuality, pain, and/or power. When the upper four seals are unlocked, a higher level of awareness is activated.

Tank®, The: It is the name given to the labyrinth used as part of the disciplines of Ramtha's School of Enlightenment. The students are taught to find the entry to this labyrinth blindfolded and move through it focusing on the Void without touching the walls or using the eyes or the senses. The objective of this discipline is to find, blindfolded, the center of the labyrinth or a room designated and representative of the Void.

Twilight®, Visualization Process: It is the process used to practice the discipline of the List or other visualization formats. The student learns to access the alpha state in the brain with focused intent in a state similar to deep sleep, yet retaining their conscious awareness.

Unknown God: The Unknown God was the single God of Ramtha's ancestors, the Lemurians. The Unknown God also represents the forgotten divinity and divine origin of the human person.

Void, the: The Source. The Void is defined as one vast nothing materially, yet all things potentially.

BIBLIOGRAPHY

Fischer, Stefan, *Hieronymus Bosch: Complete Works.* Cologne, Germany: Taschen, 2016.

Ramtha, *A Beginner's Guide to Creating Reality.* Third Edition. Yelm: JZK Publishing, a division of JZK, Inc., 2004.

Ramtha, *A Master's Reflection on the History of Humanity, Part II, Rediscovering the Pearl of Ancient Wisdom,* Second Edition. Yelm: JZK Publishing, 2017.

Ramtha, *The Brain — The Creator of Reality and a Lofty Life.* Rainier: Hun Nal Ye Publishing, 2014.

Ramtha, *Crossing the River. Fireside Series, Vol. 2, No. 1.* Yelm: JZK Publishing, a division of JZK, Inc., 2002.

Ramtha, *Only One Thing.* Audiotape 336 edition. Yelm: Ramtha Dialogues, 1996.

Ramtha, *Plane of Bliss I — On Earth As It Is In Heaven: Our Journey Through Life, Death, and Beyond.* CD-9703 and CD-9703.1 edition. Yelm: Ramtha Dialogues, 1997.

Ramtha, *Plane of Bliss II.* CD-9716 edition. Yelm: Ramtha Dialogues, 1997.

Ramtha, *Revolution of the Spirit and Mammy, the Goddess of Genesis.* Audiotape 444 edition. March 10, 2000. Yelm: Ramtha Dialogues, 2000.

Ramtha, *Selected Stories III: Shambhala — Leaving No Footprints.* Specialty Audiotape 033 edition. Yelm: Ramtha Dialogues, 1989.

Ramtha, *The Plateau for Learning.* Audiotape 268 edition. Yelm: Ramtha Dialogues, 1989.

Ramtha, *Update on Change.* Audiotape 302 edition. Yelm: Ramtha Dialogues, 1991.

Reese, William L. *Dictionary of Philosophy and Religion, Eastern and Western Thought.* Expanded ed. New York: Humanity Books, 1999.

The Complete Works of William Shakespeare. Art-Type ed. New York: Books, Inc.

Wallis, E.A., *The Egyptian Book of the Dead; the Papyrus of Ani, Egyptian Text Transliteration and Translation.* New York: Dover Publications, Inc., 1967.

Wasserman, James, *The Egyptian Book of the Dead: The Book of Going Forth by Day.* San Francisco: Chronicle Books LLC, 2008.

JZK Publishing
A Division of JZK, Inc.

P.O. Box 1210
Yelm, Washington 98597
360.458.5201
800.347.0439
www.ramtha.com
www.jzkpublishing.com

Made in the USA
San Bernardino, CA
03 May 2017